TABLE OF CONTENTS

NOTE TO THE READER

⟹◈⟸

This note to the reader is offered because the book, or parts of it, should appeal to a variety of readers. It is an ethnography using classic anthropological investigatory procedures (intensive participant observation). The book looks into the lives of one group of southern, white, male fire fighters and contains information that is of interest to anthropologists, social psychologists, regional historians, and students of mens' studies.

Fire fighters love to read about fire fighters, and not much has been written about this close knit, paramilitary group of public servants. Contained within this scientific study is an indepth story about the lives, training, and experiences of one group of fire fighters. There are parallels here for the police and the military as the demands of their occupations follow similar paths.

Some readers may choose to read this ethnography from cover to cover; other readers may choose to focus on only those chapters which meet their desires for specific information. Whatever your reasons or motivation for opening up this book, I hope it enlightens and educates.

WAITING FOR THE BIG ONE

WAITING FOR THE BIG ONE

By
Kathleen M. Cargill

Beekeeper's Press
Duluth, Minnesota

Printing: 5 4 3 2 1
Year: 00 1999 98 97 96

ISBN 0-9655503-0-3

ACKNOWLEDGEMENTS

This book is respectfully dedicated to each of the fire fighters whose cooperation made this ethnography possible. They said I could use them as a focus for my doctoral research as long as "you write the truth, and as long as we can read it." Here it is guys: read and remember the bit of history you made in Cows Crossing. I thank you very much.

Thanks also to fellow anthropologists Phyllis Chudeusz, Sandra Powers, and Susan Poats, and to psychic Donna Bohrer. You each shared my vision and provided me with more than medium support.

My thanks to Mike Busch, my husband, who said: "Does this mean we can buy an airplane?" Thanks to Maura Goessling for the pre-press production and for sharing her wit and enthusiasm during the final stages of publication. To Jennifer Huntley, photographer, for capturing the laughing, somewhat derisive me in the publicity photo: thanks for the encouragement not to be too serious. To Tom and Cosmo Rich: thanks for an inspired and colorful cover design. To the *'Cow's Crossing' Daily News* for the cover photo.

Finally I greatfully acknowledge the support and encouragement given so freely to me by Sr. Mary Richard Boo, O.S.B., Professor Emeritus; and the Sisters of the Order Of St. Benedict at The St. Scholastica Monastery, Duluth, Minnesota.

Kathleen M. Cargill
October 1996

FOREWORD

Social scientists have only recently concerned themselves with the study of American fire fighters. The present research explores the functioning of the fire fighting/emergency rescue service in a southern city called Cows Crossing. Specifically, group cohesiveness, attitudes and value systems are important areas of investigation directly related to job performance, job satisfaction and family relations. Through a focus on formal training and informal group dynamics, both stress and ritualized coping processes are identified. These latter contribute to the social solidarity and cohesive functioning of the unit.

A holistic approach is used in data gathering. The data were collected over fifteen months, April 1978–July 1979. An assessment of the research problem was completed after five months of almost daily observation and conversation with informants. Observation of informal group interaction and work routines continued throughout the study. Participation in and observation of formal training occurred in the eighth month. A survey of the fire fighters and their wives was conducted in the fourteenth month.

The theoretical orientation is drawn from Radcliffe-Brown's functionalism and Victor Turner's use of functionalism to discuss ritual processes. Reference is made to rituals of affliction.

Analysis of the intragroup dynamics indicate a breakdown in morale. This resulted largely from constraints in officers' leadership, and from the takeover by a clique of fire fighters who informally established the group's norms, which determined who remains a fire fighter at that station. The organizational problems add stress to a hazardous occupation. However, stress is mitigated and group solidarity is maintained through group ritual processes.

Recommendations for re-establishing morale are drawn from respondents' remarks. These recommendations include a return to a strict paramilitary structure which clearly delineates the duties of officers and men, the development of a strong leader, the re-opening of channels of communication and the replacement of outdated equipment.

The implications of this research are clear: (1) methods may be developed to structure and promote group cohesiveness as they relate to job effectiveness within the fire service, and (2) the findings may be used to formulate in-service training programs to address problems of intragroup social relations as they affect job performance in military, paramilitary and non-military groups.

1

INTRODUCTION

This research examines the intragroup social structure of one southern, rural fire fighting/emergency rescue service. It describes the job of fire fighting as interpreted by the study group, and examines the group cohesion, individual attitudes and value systems which are related to job performance, job satisfaction and family relations. The ritual processes used to mitigate stress and maintain group cohesion are a special focus of the research.

Fire fighting offers an interesting setting for anthropological study. These fire fighters are a group of men whose job requires that they face hazards daily and that they do so as a team, rather than as independent agents. They are subjected often to extreme physical, psychological and social stress which may have a deleterious effect on them (Hegge *et al,* 1979). Of interest is their individual adaptation to stress and the manner in which stress and its mitigation affects their relationships with others in the group. This research pinpoints areas of physical, emotional and social stress and the ways the men have of mitigating stress. The research also examines the men's perceptions of their role in caring for other people and the reactions of members of their community to them. These perceptions and reactions say something about group pride and *esprit de corps,* both of which are characteristics of a cohesive unit.

The group is also homogeneous (rural, southern white males) and is not representative of the rural southern population, nor of other groups of fire fighters. The research examines whether homogeneity is perceived by the fire fighters as necessary for group cohesion. Also it is interesting to examine this group before it is pressured to change by social and legal forces, and before these changes introduce new stress into the group.

For the purpose of this study I derived specific objectives to achieve a systematic description of the job, stress, social structure and coping processes. These objectives are: to elucidate the formal training procedures by which a group of disparate individuals become a cohesive working unit with shared values and attitudes

(Woods, 1974); to delineate the informal socialization dynamics which build a cohesive functioning unit; to relate the fire fighting/emergency rescue unit to its external social support system; and to delineate factors in the community (e.g., socioeconomic status, residential patterning, racial segregation) which are important to the fire fighters' role definition and to their job performance.

To fulfill the above objectives I derived four interrelated hypotheses during the course of the data collection: (1) group cohesiveness will be fostered by rigorous, specialized training which emphasizes teamwork (Bourne, 1970); (2) group cohesiveness will be fostered by informal socialization rituals practiced on the job (Turner, 1968, 1969; Bourne, 1970); (3) group cohesiveness will reflect community standards and shared attitudes about family life, social class and ethnic group (Warren, 1972; Olmsted and Hare, 1978; LeMasters, 1975; Niederhoffer, 1978); and (4) group cohesiveness may enhance or detract from the effectiveness of fire fighting/emergency rescue operations (Barth, 1969).

The hypotheses are tested against a database of information from in-service training and education; life histories; attitudes and role definition of the study group; interpersonal dynamics among the fire fighters focusing on job related physical and emotional stress and their mitigation; interpersonal dynamics between fire fighters and their families focusing on the effects of job related stress on family life; and attitudes and values concerning socioeconomic and ethnic dimensions within the community.

The writings of Radcliffe-Brown and Victor Turner greatly influenced my thinking during the theoretical development of the research and as I examined the fire fighters' social structure and their use of ritual processes. I also derived an understanding of social structure from the writings of Ralph Turner and of ritual processes from van Gennep, Chapple and Leaf.

The concept of mechanical solidarity is used because the fire fighters are concerned with maintaining group cohesiveness through the cooperation of its members. With mechanical solidarity in mind, I identified group norms, values, sentiments and beliefs. Small group boundary maintenance is established through group norms by which feelings of in-group and out-group develop. I applied the concept of mechanical solidarity to the fire fighters in a parallel manner to Ralph Turner's study of a group of disaster victims. The fire fighters may be defined as a cohesive unit in part because of their shared sentiments toward outsiders which develop under stress.

The concept of functionalism defined by Radcliffe-Brown and later utilized by Victor Turner is used to examine the role of ritual processes in the maintenance of group cohesion. As used here, Radcliffe-Brown defined the "function of any recurrent activity . . . is the part it plays in the social life as a whole and therefore the contribution it makes to the maintenance of the structural continuity" (Radcliffe-Brown, 1961:180). Ritual processes continue to be important even in an increasingly secular world (van Gennep, 1960). There is a relationship between ritual behavior and the dynamics of individual and group life among the fire fighters (van Gennep, 1960; Chapple, 1942; Turner, 1969). Life crises affect both individuals and the people around them, and when these crises create group disequilibrium it requires the intervention of ritual ceremonies to re-establish group solidarity. I applied the processes and models of liminality and communitas developed by Turner (1969) to the fire fighters in order to understand the intragroup dynamics which revolve around the ritual ceremonies. Rites of passage, rituals of status elevation/reversal and rites of affliction (redress) are cited specifically in an attempt to understand the role of four ritual processes utilized by the study group.

The fire fighters' ritual processes are complex and dynamic. They incorporate many variables each time they occur. No one notion, theory or model on ritual process perfectly fits any one of the rituals. Therefore I combine Victor Turner's functionalist discussion of ritual with Leaf's information theory to more fully describe the role ritual plays in the study group.

Anthropology provides a unique way of understanding small groups. Thus the same procedure can be used to conceptualize and study fire fighters as was used in earlier studies of the police and military combat units (Bourne, 1970; Caiden, 1977; Caputo, 1977; Niederhoffer, 1978). Groups of fire fighters have been the subjects of job performance analyses (Schau, 1974; Miller, 1976; Rush, 1977), however, social scientists have completed few natural group studies as those by Smith (1972, 1976) who is a fire fighter, and Woods (1974). Fire fighters are of anthropological interest in the morphological sense (e.g., the structure of their social system); in the functional sense (e.g., the manner in which the social system is maintained); and in the cognitive sense (e.g., the manner in which the system and its rituals are understood by the members themselves).

The fire fighters are viewed as a small group rather than as individual fire fighters or as members of a broader group called American fire fighters. Their small group in its natural setting is of manageable size and lent itself to qualitative data gathering techniques. The focus of this research is on an ethnographic understanding of the perceptions shared by the fire fighters about group structure and on the rituals they use to maintain it. The research variables are not experimentally manipulated as a psychologist might do in an examination of a single fire fighter. Nor did I approach the subjects as a sociologist might by surveying a cross section of fire fighters in the United States. Instead, the primary objective is to describe this small group as people who use a particular "system of rules, goals, value techniques . . . socialization procedures and decision procedure" (Diesing, 1971:5–6).

A holistic anthropological approach, intensive participant observation and the personal approach were used in data gathering over the fifteen months from April, 1978 to July, 1979. Initially these methods allowed me to establish rapport with the members of the study group, to allow a measure of empathy, or "we" feeling to develop in me and to allow a bond of trust to develop between individual fire fighters and me. These approaches are crucial because rapport with the fire fighters and the trust of the key informants is essential to obtaining clear and valid field data. The study could not have been completed without these two ingredients.

This is a natural group study and although working hypotheses were derived, the men were not brought together for the purpose of proving or disproving a predetermined hypothesis. However, two research instruments were utilized at the conclusion of the observation period to verify observations already recorded and to provide a vehicle for the fire fighters to supplement the data with personal comment. These were a written questionnaire and a structured oral interview. The technique of following recorded observations with interviews is basic to anthropology and its strength lies in its corroboration of observed data. Also, the structured interviews conducted at the end of an observation period are less intrusive than if they are administered during the early stages of observation.

The participant observer method and the personal approach were used in this research because they allow the researcher to discover patterns of behavior which the group members may not be consciously aware of, and to discover group attitudes and perspectives. These approaches were utilized because they allow for systematic data gathering as well as provide the latitude I needed to discover what the fire fighters were about—their social structure and its maintenance.

As an anthropologist using these holistic field techniques I lived in the same community as the study group and took the time to know them by recording their activities over several months. Also, the fieldwork situation allowed me "to personally ascertain the satisfactoriness of a description and the pattern derived from a series of descriptions" (Honigman, 1976:245). Honigman's encouragement of traditional anthropological inquiries–"a configuration of personal abilities and other resources" (1976:243)–is appealing to me as a social scientist and entirely appropriate to the study of a small group. Finally, as is traditional in anthropology the study group and its community are brought to life through the use of the ethnographic present.

The implications of the research are clear. First, the descriptive material may be used to formulate specific, testable hypotheses so that more specific, perhaps problem-oriented, research may be conducted within similar groups. Such groups might be military combat units, oil rig crews assigned to ocean duty, the police, prison guards and so forth. Second, the findings may be used to formulate in-service training programs to address problems of intragroup social relations as they affect job performance within the fire service. Third, methods may be developed to structure and promote group cohesiveness as it relates to the effectiveness of variously structured fire departments within the United States Fire Service.

The research reported here was done in Cows Crossing (a pseudonym), a city in a southern state with a population a little over 9,000. The social structure of the community is differentiated by ethnic group and class. Cows Crossing's economy is based on industry, recreation and agriculture. Its early economic well-being depended upon the winter tourist business and the cypress lumber industry. At the present time, the economy is based largely on manufacturing, the citrus industry and the tourists who are drawn to the large river and many lakes in the county.

The Cows Crossing Fire department (CCFD) has five officers and thirteen men. It is the largest department in the county and the only paid one. The fire fighters are all white southern males engaged in a highly skilled, stressful and hazardous occupation. Nearly all the men grew up in Cows Crossing; all are residents now. They identify themselves first as fire fighters, second as southerners and third as members of the working class. The men have functioned in a dual capacity as fire fighters and as emergency medical technicians (EMT's) or paramedics since 1973. As fire fighters they serve an area of 5.5 square miles, and as emergency rescue teams they serve an area of about 600 square miles. Although the study group is referred to only as fire fighters throughout the research, their dual function must be kept in mind. Research among these men posed some interesting fieldwork problems which were resolved by using fieldwork techniques basic to anthropological inquiry. The field problems and the research methodology I used to study the fire fighters is discussed in the following chapter.

2

THE RESEARCH METHODOLOGY

The research methodology, which is derived from the holistic approach of anthropology, allows for data gathering in which demographic, historic and organizational materials can be integrated with field notes and with interview data. Participant observation is the main technique for data collection and the personal approach is used to gain entry to the study group and to establish rapport with research subjects and with the key informants. These are essentially the techniques which underlie this study.

The data were collected over a fifteen month period from April, 1978 to July, 1979. A feasibility assessment was completed after five months of almost daily observation and conversations with key informants. Observation of group interaction and work routines continued throughout the study. Participation in and observation of formal fire fighting training took place principally in the seventh and eighth months. Finally, an extensive survey using written and oral interviews of the fire fighters and their wives was conducted in the fourteenth month. The research stages outlined below overlapped in time, therefore Table 1 was constructed for easy reference.

The Fieldwork Situation I:
Feasibility of Participant Observation

Field Problems/Development of Key Informants:
April–August, 1978

The feasibility assessment was made in order to identify research problems and to formulate a research design based on theoretical and methodological materials. The result of these initial observations was the establishment of rapport with the study group so that key informants could be developed. Several aspects of the participant observation approach were considered during the feasibility assessment as well as throughout the observation period. These are: (1) the advantages and disadvantages of using

Table 1
The Research Methodology:
Time Frame

STAGE OF RESEARCH	TIME FRAME
The Fieldwork Situation I: Feasibility of Participant Observation	1978
Field Problems	April–August
Identifying Key Informants	April–December
Obtaining Permission	September
The Fieldwork Situation II: Chronology of Participant Observation	1978
Daily Routine	September–October
Social Events	Ongoing
Fire College	
Basic 200 Hours Course	October–November
Smokedivers	November
Local Training, Cows Crossing, FL	Ongoing
Fire Season, Cows Crossing, FL	October–March
The Fieldwork Situation III: The Research Instruments	1979
The Questionnaires (written)	May
The Interview Schedule (oral)	June
Analysis and Composition	June, 1979–Present

participant observation in a natural group study; (2) the merits of using the personal approach along with participant observation, including the fluctuation of my role *vis à vis* the study group; (3) the process of choosing key informants; (4) the validity and reliability of the data gathered through the use of participant observation field methods; and (5) the fieldworker used in a manner similar to a research instrument. Also considered are issues of reciprocity, countertransference or reactivity, and field ethics when using key informants.

Advantages/disadvantages of participant observation. A research methodology which combines participant observation, the personal approach and other resources appeared to be the most appropriate way to begin research on fire fighters. Participant observation allowed me to approach the study group on a personal level with the least intrusion possible. As noted, recording the affects of informal relationships on group cohesion was one research goal. Participant observation allowed me to gather anecdotal material and data on the patterns of behavior within the study group that pertained to cohesiveness.

Participant observation is a flexible technique which allows for different degrees of involvement with the study group: (1) as an observer only, (2) as a researcher where the researcher directs conversations to specific topics, or (3) as a participant in the event being observed (Gans, 1962:338).

Each role was used to elicit different types of data, but the third role was the most useful in this small group study. In the first role (observer) I was able to watch fire and rescue operations. These were excellent opportunities to record and photograph examples of team work and to understand the hazards of fire fighting and emergency rescue procedures. This researcher role was used primarily in two instances: (1) when specific pieces of information were needed to clarify my understanding of a problem, event or technique, and (2) during the formal interviews at the conclusion of the observation period. With the third role, I functioned as part of the group in social events, formal training sessions and in general conversation with the men. At these times the men appeared more relaxed and discussed such things as their families, their attitudes towards their jobs, other fire fighters, community events and their role in the community.

The participant observation method presented some problems in data gathering which had to be resolved before or during the observation period. Two problems which Gans (1962:340) noted in his research of urban working class people paralleled those I faced: gaining entry, and acceptance as an outsider. Initial entry was facilitated because I had established an intimate relationship with one of the fire fighters and as "his woman" had a right to come to the station. At this stage I made no attempt to establish myself as a social scientist, but rather just as a college student. However, gaining acceptance was more of a problem for me. After living in Cows Crossing for four years, I was perceived to be a member of the upper-middle class because I was a member of the family that was the largest single employer in town. That social position plus my northern upbringing, my sex, my educational level and my lack of knowledge about fire fighting made me an outsider. Further, the group had well established boundaries based on sex, upbringing, knowledge of and pride in fire fighting. The differences between the study group and me were perceived by the men to be reasons for preventing my intrusion.

They thought that I would treat them in an off-handed and superior manner because of my perceived social class standing. Their discomfort in my presence was readily apparent and initially I sought to reassure them through repeated individual conversations. Acceptance was facilitated when I told the men of my own working class background and when I expressed the values and priorities inherent in that social class. For example, I talked about my background by explaining what my father and mother did for a living, by assuring them that I had attended public schools in a rural area, and by talking about how hard it was to work in order to attend college. This voluntary sharing of my own life history apparently reduced the perceived differences between us making the men more comfortable in my presence and more open to sharing their own life's experiences. Also I did not flaunt my education. Knowledge and opinions I expressed on any subject were proffered after permission to speak had been given to me. In that way, the men had the option of listening or not.

My acceptance was enhanced also by the enthusiasm of Jack Brown, the assistant chief. He supported the research project and intervened in the initial stage of the fieldwork by assuring the men about me as a person. Some of the fire fighters expressed concern that I would "talk down" to them presumably because I was "upper class" and "better educated." Jack responded that, "She may have gone to college and she may be a classy broad, but she doesn't know a damned thing about fire fighting and that's what she's here to learn. So why don't you guys just talk to her on your level and see what happens." Fortunately the fire fighters took their assistant chief's advice and channels of communication between members of the study group and me opened during the feasibility assessment.

Finally, because I lacked knowledge about fire fighting I also placed myself in a role of student or almost that of a rookie fire fighter. This provided an avenue for the fire fighters to teach me

— to be, in fact, the better educated. This, too, reduced some of the problems imposed by perceived status differences.

Merits of the personal approach. Group acceptance of me as a researcher was negotiated in two stages through the use of the personal approach, an approach which includes many of the same interpersonal processes used to establish friendships between two individuals: the sharing of ideas, listening, and exchanging favors. The two stages may be labeled: (1) my acceptance as a woman by the terms the fire fighters used to relate to women in general, and (2) my acceptance as a professional person who viewed fire fighting and fire fighters in a positive light.

The initial role was outlined for me by the men's reactions to other women. They accorded me respect and courtesy, which is an initial response to any "new woman." They did not "joke around," and avoided profane or obscene language. By trying to establish rapport with a few men at a time, I allowed them to relate to me in ways already familiar to them. That is, I tried to gain the acceptance of the group by convincing at least a few men that I was a "traditional woman." Once this "feminine" role was established, I began to work toward the role of "sister to men"—a woman who is a friend but not a sexual target (Nader, 1970). Such a role was perceived to be less threatening to the wives of the fire fighters, and provided a way for the men to respond to me without sexual overtones.

In the role of the "new woman," I was initially on display at the fire station and was evaluated by the men. From their criticisms of the behavior of other fire fighters' wives, I knew I was expected to be quiet, not bother the fire fighters and to remember that the fire station was a place of male business. By following the fire fighters' directions I attempted to reduce reactivity and increase my chances of being accepted by the men.

The role of traditional woman, as interpreted by these men, had several important characteristics. They wanted "their women" to be ladies who did not swear, tell off-color jokes, who performed women's work well, and who did not comment negatively on anything seen or heard at the fire station. This last was particularly important because the fire station was "her man's world," and women were perceived to be marginal actors by both fire fighters and by the women. By conforming to their concept of a traditional home maker eventually I was accepted on that basis.

As indicated above, I was also "the rookie's woman." Ron Emmet was the newest member of the fire fighting squad. His personal and professional status increased with seniority, and as he proved himself to be a good fire fighter/EMT. As his acceptance increased, so did mine because I was seen, in part, as "his" or as an extension of him. Later, as my role shifted to that of a social scientist, so did the rookie's role shift. Occasionally Ron acted as a go-between explaining certain aspects of the research to the men. In particular, some men questioned him about the content of the research questionnaires. He told them about the categories of questions and generally discussed the research, but he made it very clear that he did not have access to the field notes nor any advance notice of the questions to be included on the research instruments. At no time during the research did Ron ask to see my field notes, nor ask to listen to the taped interviews, nor read the answers to the research questionnaires.

After these entry level problems were resolved or smoothed over, and the role of traditional woman was established, I sought permission to do the research. The fire chief and the assistant chief presented me as a social scientist to the fire fighters. Afterwards I was perceived in this new light as a professional who had specific reasons for observing operations at the fire station. Although I was still an outsider, the shift in roles allowed the fire fighters to help me become an informed outsider, which is an adaptation from "informed stranger" (Gusfield, 1960:102). This gave the men a reason for speaking to me even though I am a woman. As the research progressed, men other than the key informants offered information without prompting, and appeared to enjoy the idea of being studied.

The shift in role was also necessary to make the project more meaningful to the subjects, and to insure that the reasons for my presence were not obscured. Eventually I was perceived as a friend to fire fighters and as a person who had a specific reason for being at the station. Finally, a shift in role was necessary so that I might be placed in a better position to view the organizational structure and its problems from the perspective of the members of the study group.

Field ethics and key informants. By incorporating the study group's value of honesty into my research scheme, I carefully chose key informants to resolve a problem Gans (1962:242) thought was inherent in the use of participant observation. He worries about the ethics of a method which he believes does not provide a means for a researcher to fully share information about herself with the group. However, I agree with Powdermaker (1966) who presents an opposing view. To establish rapport with the key informants, to increase my empathy with the group and to increase my identification with the family of fire fighters, I used the fire fighters' system of reciprocity and their pattern of joking to share information about myself. Reciprocity, or gift exchange, was used as a friendly gesture, to open communication, or to obligate a fire fighter to me. For example, some fire fighters asked me to get printed material or other information from agencies outside the county. Some of this material pertained to personal problems while other materials were related to academic goals. On other occasions the fire fighters helped me move my belongings to new residences in exchange for home cooked meals. Reciprocity was a common practice among the men who often said, "You owe me one," and was a way for me to make myself useful to the group by establishing a functional role *vis à vis* individual men.

The pattern of reciprocity continually developed throughout the study as increasingly complex exchanges were made. The fire fighters appeared to like the qualities of openness and a willingness to talk, therefore I remained open to relationships with all the men throughout the study. Some exchange processes between the fire fighters and me expanded the bounds of friendship into a quasi-therapeutic transaction. Many shared personal experiences, problems and confidences with me. In exchange, I listened without expressing judgements, asked questions to keep the conversation going or, on occasion, offered advice or practical solutions to problems. Lundberg saw this "therapeutic exchange . . . (as) . . . confirming for the informant's identity and feelings of self-worth" (1968:42). The fire fighters and I perceived this process as something which friends do for each other.

To further establish rapport with the group and to allow them to get to know me, I participated in some of the jokes they told or played on each other. Joking has a practical use among groups which use it as a measure of acceptance of new members or to aggravate established members of the group. This was the case with the fire fighters for whom the ability to take a joke was important. Horseplay, practical jokes and verbal jokes were a daily occurrence at the station. A rookie was often the object of practical jokes or verbal barbs. However, as he became a member of the group, he was allowed to "pay back" the joker in kind. As the research progressed, many pranks and jokes were played on me "to see if she could take it." I did take it; I "paid back" some of the men for their jokes and a joking relationship rapidly developed between some of the men and me. Such relationships were not only personally gratifying to me, they were also a clear statement of companionability (Richardson, 1978:106). Further, joking facilitated data gathering because it made me welcome at the station and provided one channel of communication for the men. The men felt that if I could take a joke, I was "all right" and it was acceptable to talk to me about other subjects. As a bond of trust between the study group and me was fostered by joking, I became less of an outsider.

Honesty and trust were highly valued by group members. The men's questions about my activities always were discussed with them. When they asked why a particular piece of information was necessary, they were told how their answers might relate to the research problem. Also, as stated, I was open to relationships with all the men, but to a greater extent with the men targeted as key informants. By letting the informants watch me watching them at the station, and by letting them get to know me through social events at the station and in my home, I provided clear channels of communication for all the men.

Ethical considerations regarding the development of informant relationships were in the forefront throughout the research, but particularly during the feasibility assessment, or the "getting to know you" stage. Friendship with many of the men was the happy result of the research. However, as Pfifferling (1978:3) and Oliver-Smith (1979:78–80) have stated, in studying any group issues of friendship and the definition of friendship should be of major concern to an anthropologist who must walk a narrow line between being a friend and using a friend to collect information. The subject group has to be protected precisely because as friendships develop, the knowledge that they are being studied will fade into the background. To maintain professional ethics and to retain friends, I continually and clearly articulated the goals of the research (Oliver-Smith, personal communication). Further, I chose not to include in the data analysis those discussions of a strictly personal nature that would have compromised the professional standing of any individual fire fighter (Pfifferling, 1978:5). In addition, the inclusion of too many details about the men's individual lives would have been a personal and professional breech of confidentiality, and would have cast serious doubt on my credibility. These professional ethics mirrored those group ethics held by the men: that is, "what goes on at the station, stays at the station."

Generally, all the fire fighters were informants who could be counted upon to provide descriptions of station routine, rescue events, fire incidents, and hazardous materials incidents. Men who were proficient in specific fire related subjects were questioned intermittently to clarify my observations. Opinions of men who openly and consistently praised the fire department were contrasted with those opinions from men who openly and consistently criticized the department. Men who represented these extremes often were marginal to the daily intragroup processes, but their opinions provided useful perspectives (Wax, 1960:93).

The development of several key informants was essential to this ethnographic research because the "man's world" of the fire station did not provide an official place for a woman. For example, the instances of group ritual were closed to me, therefore key informants were used to carefully describe the rituals, their reason for occurring, the men's feelings about the rituals and the implications of those processes. By relying on informants, I also received information on unusual occurrences during the ritual or on some outstanding action between one or two participants.

Four men were consistently willing to fill in the gaps in information and responded to detailed and often personal questions. The choice and development of informants shifted as the research progressed, depending upon the reliability of informants' previous information and their areas of expertise. Some informants were more willing to discuss the interrelationships among the men and to provide personal information about their own and others' lives. Others were able to teach me about fire fighting and emergency rescue. Still others could be counted on to inform me about upcoming events, such as fire and smoke drills.

Ron Emmet was the first informant and introduced me to the fire service and to the Cows Crossing Fire Department. Two men were added towards the conclusion of the feasibility assessment: one was Jack Brown, the assistant chief, the other was Joe Smith, a senior fire fighter who was identified as a leader among the men. In later months, "J.W." Jones, another senior fire fighter, who was promoted to the rank of captain during the observation period, emerged as a key informant. The fact that officers were included among the key informants posed less of a problem than it might have. The officers were close to their men and there were few barriers between them such as those which exist in highly structured military settings. For example, officers and men slept in the same barracks. The officers also had come up through the ranks recently enough to remember the problems they had as fire fighters. Further, the officers were able to discuss the special pressures they faced as leaders. The officer-informants placed no restrictions on me nor on the fire fighters who wished to speak to me.

The key informants were not marginal to the group. For example, the man who was the greatest source of information on small group interaction emerged as the principal informant from an unpleasant incident which occurred in May, 1978. A difference of opinion developed between Joe and Tommy Lee and me, when I inadvertently stepped out of my role as "traditional woman." The two men were involved in some horseplay at the station and I commented in jest on the situation. Tommy Lee was offended at the remark and Joe Smith took it as a joke. Joe served as mediator between Tommy and me, settled the disagreement and emerged as a valuable informant. Subsequent long conversations with Joe resulted in a marked increase in the group's acceptance of me.

While serendipity was a factor in the development of Joe as a key informant, others were chosen more consciously to offer a balance among the informants. Men who were close friends to each other were not both chosen as key informants to avoid the appearance of my alliance with one clique against another. Fire fighters as well as officers were chosen in order to avoid the appearance of my alliance with officers against the fire fighters.

Validity and reliability of key informants. Validity and reliability are always critical issues when working with key informants. Dean and Whyte ask simply, "How do you know if the informant is telling the truth?" They outline several questions a fieldworker can ask to check for inaccuracies or distortions by informants: (1) Is the account plausible?, (2) Has the informant been reliable in the past?, (3) Does the fieldworker understand the informant's mental set (where he is coming from)?, and (4) How does this informant's account compare with other accounts of the same event (Dean and Whyte, 1958:36–37). These questions provided a consistent impetus for me to cross check informants' reports and to compare their reports with field notes.

Cross checking informants' reports sounds more facile than it really is. Informants themselves must be assessed for any "ulterior motives" they may have in reporting an event. The situation in which I solicited information had to be perceived in a positive way by the informant in order to avoid "bars to spontaneity." I had to be alert to any "desires to please" which the informant might have (Dean and Whyte, 1958:35). For example, information about or analyses of interpersonal dynamics and group rituals were often very personal. Therefore, to identify potentially biased material, or to check that which was suspected of being biased, informants' reports were constantly cross checked.

Reactivity is a major source of possible bias in fieldwork because the fieldworker has an influence on the field situation. The key informants may have tried to impress me or "put their best foot forward." Sometimes this was not a problem, as when I elicited factual data about fire fighting techniques. In fact, in order to allow the men to "put their best foot forward" I arranged the research so that formal, objective, detailed information about fire fighting and fire fighter training were obtained first.

Reactivity might have been a problem when I elicited data on departmental problems or individual attitudes on various subjects. I had to watch for over eager informants who might have tried to filter information so that I got only what I needed to prove my hypothesis. Also during general discussions with the men I tried to express neutral opinions so that the men would continue to tell me what they thought and not just react to my statements or opinions.

In this research reactivity was minimized by the length of the project. Over a period of several months the men became less concerned with my presence and with the research. They did not forget why I was there, but as the fire season came, they were too busy to worry about me. They had to get on with their business, most of which they could not hide. Time, combined with the participant observation method appeared to be the best defense against reactivity. Also, throughout the study I remained as unobtrusive as humanly possible.

Countertransference is related to reactivity. It is described by LaBarre (1948;967) as the effect of a fieldworker's own feelings towards the study group being reflected back to her in their attitudes towards her. I dealt with fieldwork frustration or negative feelings about the study group by leaving the station or talking to other professionals about research problems or the idiosyncrasies of the study group. It was important for me to get away from the intensity of the research situation to gain perspective as well as to reduce reactivity or countertransference.

Bias can also be introduced by "idiosyncratic factors" which cause "the informant to express only one facet of his reactions to a subject" (Dean and Whyte, 1958:35). The life history of each informant in the study, his prejudices and attitudes as well as his position relative to the other men had to be considered when assessing the value of his information.

With the participant observer role and through the use of informants, I solicited everyone's opinion with the result that more data was collected than anticipated. There was no "one opinion" on any given subject for which data was solicited. However, with the detailed reporting from key informants and the in-depth interviews of each fire fighter, there emerged patterns of feelings and perceptions, patterns of opinions and patterns of behavior. It was these patterns of behavior that made up the focus of this research on interpersonal dynamics within this paramilitary organizational structure.

Fieldworker as a research instrument. One final point must be presented about the validity of the data collected through participant observation and the personal approach. Honigman states the fieldworker "personally ascertains the satisfactoriness of a description and the patterns derived from a series of descriptions" (1976:245). This calls for "considerable intuition, speculative ability and speculative freedom as well as abundant, detailed data" (Honigman, 1976:247). Von Mering (personal communication) calls this intuitive process a recognition of "felt facts."

I used myself as a research instrument and had confidence in such a usage. Many anthropologists such as Mead, Bateson and LaBarre were influenced by Freud's psychoanalytical theories presented through Dollard and Sapir's culture and personality classes in the 1930's (LaBarre, 1958:279). They suggest that in order for an anthropologist to fully understand any study group, she had to first understand her own human potential and limitations (LaBarre, 1958:280, 302). They recommend that anthropologists be psychoanalyzed before entering the field. I had confidence, however, in my own ability to sense when data reported to me were incorrect or biased or when my own interpretation "did not feel right."

On a professional level, I had developed good data gathering techniques through the use of participant observation, the personal approach, reciprocity and through the development of research instruments in two previous fieldwork situations (Albert *et al*, 1977; Cargill-Mazer, 1978:41). Finally, I prepared myself for the research in Cows Crossing by having lived in the community for four years and by being familiar with the community's values and mores (Stephenson and Greer, 1981).

In summary, participant observation is not a perfect method and only I can be held accountable for the validity and reliability of the qualitative data which I collected. The conclusions drawn are only as reliable as the field notes (Honigman, 1976:248; Langness, 1965:45). Further, much of the uniqueness of the approach is based on the personal qualities of the investigator. The participant observer "is aided by her (sic) senses and reason as well as by intuition . . . " (Bruyn, 1963:231). The personal approach and participant observation, however, are useful in research whose goal is describing a way of life, tracing relationships between patterns of culture or interpreting the meaning of ritual within a social structure (Honigman, 1976:249).

Obtaining Permission: September, 1978.

In early September, 1978, the assistant chief, Jack Brown, was approached with a proposal to study the Cows Crossing Fire Department. I told him the study would involve observing the fire fighters' formal training, specific orientation and training procedures used at the station, and the role of the fire department in the community. I explained that the group was of interest because its profession required small teams of men to work, live, and play together under alternating periods of great physical and mental stress and boredom. Because the group was one of the last of a kind with its all white male paramilitary structure, it was important to describe the group in context of its community and its role in the emergency health care system, before it was forced to change.

The assistant chief expressed a desire to see someone write about fire fighters because he thought the profession was not well understood and that the men were not given the respect they deserved. He agreed to encourage the fire chief to allow me to talk to the men, to observe the daily routine, and to attend drills and fire operations. He added that I might not like what I saw and heard. Jack was assured that the object of the research was to describe a way of life, not to judge it. He further stated that the study would be terminated if I got in the way at a fire scene or if my actions endangered the life of any of the fire fighters. I agreed to these restrictions.

In mid-September I attended a regular Wednesday night meeting to explain the proposed research to the fire fighters, the volunteers and to the officers. I explained that the anonymity of the community, the department and the individuals was assured by the use of pseudonyms and by the caveat that participation in the interviews would be voluntary. The assistant chief for the volunteers, Pete Byrd, asked about the hypothesis for the study, and was told that this was a descriptive study with no single hypothesis.

At the conclusion of the presentation, formal permission for the study was granted by the two highest ranking officers and the tacit approval of the men was granted. Clearance for the study was based on the recognition of at least two levels of decision-making: the officers and the men. The men granted only tacit approval that night for two reasons: (1) not enough of the men knew me well enough to trust me completely, and (2) some suspicion was generated by a statement made during the presentation that the study group was of interest because of its all white, southern male make up. The following day, I went to the station to talk to one man who had openly expressed his doubts. He was a well respected fire fighter and his support was important. He and "other men" feared the dissertation would be an expose of a group of racially biased men, and were concerned that this information would reflect negatively on the fire service. The research project was re-explained, emphasizing the point that I intended to describe what I saw and not to judge the men or the department (see "unconditional regard," Lundberg, 1968:47).

Apparently this was repeated to other fire fighters, because two days later several men asked if the fire department would receive something tangible for their cooperation. The men suggested they would like a copy of whatever was written and I agreed that the fire department would receive a copy of the research. The fire fighters understood they might not like what would be written, but they claimed that as long as the truth were told, they did not have to like it.

A third stamp of approval for the study came in late October when one of the volunteers, Pete Byrd, questioned me about the study. After a brief conversation, this veteran fire fighter offered to help in any way he could. As assistant chief for the volunteers, he provided valuable information about the history of the Cows

Crossing Fire Department and about the integration and training of the volunteers into the paid fire department. His own status with the paid men as a good fire fighter helped me gain acceptance.

The Fieldwork Situation II:
A Chronology of Participant Observation

Daily Routine: September–October, 1978

With permission to complete the study, my role shifted from "the rookie's woman" to professional. This new role facilitated the formal note taking period which lasted from September, 1978 to July, 1979. Daily routine provided the structure for the intra-group dynamics, therefore each shift was observed performing its daily chores from 8 AM to 6 PM. I was allowed anywhere in the station except the barracks, and I could not spend the night at the station. I received a description and drawing of the barracks from a key informant and relied on informant reports for activities which occurred at night. Throughout the year other observations of daily routine were made a half day at a time, during the morning, the afternoon or evening. Because the station was considered a place of business, conversations with the men were reserved for afternoons and evenings when station chores were done.

Conversations were initiated or maintained with a comment or a question from me, after which I withdrew to listen to the discussion. General conversations between the men not only revealed the subjects of greatest interest to them, but revealed the nature of the relationships among them. The information collected during the talks was compared to and used to elaborate on data obtained from the structured interviews. Conversational data also provided answers to questions which were difficult to ask in a short survey instrument.

Social Events: Ongoing

There were ten or more social events in which I participated with the fire fighters, categorized as: (a) station events, (b) community events, or (3) individual socializing. Station events included shift dinners which were on Sundays or major holidays, and department events such as the annual Mother's Day dinner, at which paid and volunteer fire fighters and their wives or mothers joined a few community and business leaders for dinner at the station. The extent of the fire fighters' participation in the preparations for the events was recorded, in addition to a list of those who attended, and the way the men felt about them. These events gave me a feeling for the relationship that existed between the community and the fire department.

The fire department participated in community events such as holiday parades, rodeos, fireworks on July 4th, boat races and football games. During these events I sat with the men in the rescue units or on the fire apparatus and observed how the men interacted with the crowds and how they handled emergencies.

Fire and smoke training drills also functioned as community social events. They served a community public relations function for the fire department as well as a means through which I interacted with the wives and family of the fire fighters. The individual socializing I did with the fire fighters was recorded because these conversations often turned to problems at the station, fire or rescue events, or to the interpersonal relations between the men.

Fire College: October–November, 1978

Six times per year the State Fire College conducts a 5-week Basic 200 Hours Course for entry level fire fighters. It also offers a one-week Smokedivers Course designed for fire fighters with three or more years of experience. I obtained permission from the training coordinator to attend the classes, to take pictures of the practical training and to administer questionnaires to the students. The objective of the observations was to discover if formal training had any bearing on the team effort necessary in fire fighting and rescue operations.

The fire college welcomed the opportunity to have an independent researcher learn about the formal training and suggested that participant observation was the only way I could obtain an accurate perspective. Library materials and in-house publications were placed at my disposal. Both the administration and the instructional staff requested a copy of the research in exchange for allowing the observations to be made.

The instructors welcomed me, introduced me to the classes as an observer and allowed me to participate in class drills and field drills ("evolutions"). Rapport with some of the assistant instructors came only after I had overcome their ill-feelings toward a psychologist who was involved with an on-going study of training standards. He refused to participate in the training, or, as they put it, "get his hands dirty," and his apparent lack of empathy for fire fighters irked the instructors. The assistant instructors were convinced of my sincerity because I participated in the field drills. One instructor was impressed because I presented myself neither "as a lady or a fireman, but as a colleague."

There were only two instances in which the administration directly attempted to influence the outcome of the observations. One administrator tried to interpret events or the outcome of training procedures to me. He was anxious that I note the team effort, brotherhood, and group support of men who were having trouble with certain field drills. On the second occasion, another administrator offered to help "write the report, especially since things written about firemen sometimes turn the firemen off. Just the most innocent statement can be misunderstood." I politely refused these offers and restated my purpose which was to describe the training and not to evaluate it.

Basic 200 Hours Course. Twenty-three men from various fire stations in the state were observed during four weeks of the 5-week Basic 200 Hours Course. It was a class designed to train entry level fire fighters in the state. A Certification of Compliance with state standards was issued at the successful completion of the course, and the certificate was a job requirement in Cows Crossing. I was introduced to the class by the instructor as a professional who would be observing the training sessions. Initially the students perceived me as a "lady," and modified their behavior, avoiding profanity and off-color jokes. I de-emphasized my role as a lady to these students so that barriers in communication would be broken as quickly as possible. I did not respond negatively to the swearing and off-color jokes of the instructors, and as soon as the students perceived that I was not offended by the instructor's behavior, they appeared to relax and include me in their conversations.

The students in this class were administered a General Questionnaire developed at the end of the fifth week. There were 40 questions, 10 of which were open-ended and 30 were forced choice. The questions elicited demographic data as well as data on education and training, fire fighting experience, present or desired employment, the qualities of a good fire fighter and a brief exploration of the stresses involved in fire fighting. Ten men completed the questionnaire out of a possible 22 students.

Because of their low response rate, data were used only to devise a research instrument for use with the study group in Cows Crossing.

Smokedivers. During the week long Smokedivers Class I observed morning drills, then participated in many of the evolutions, or graduated drills, in the afternoon. The stated purpose for the training was to hone techniques and to provide a controlled environment in which a man was pushed to his physical and mental limits. The men were taught to recognize their weaknesses and to work through them. They were further encouraged to communicate with each other continually, to trust each other and to trust their equipment.

The instructors introduced me as a graduate student interested in observing and participating in the advanced training process for research purposes. It was decided that I would participate in the Smokedivers' evolutions because this was an experience for which most fire fighters waited years. It was also an important way of establishing useful contacts for pretesting a questionnaire.

In order to participate in the evolutions, I donned a four piece protective suit, called "bunker gear," which was provided by the college: boots, pants, coat and helmet. For most of the work, an air tank and breathing mask were used. The protective gear and the breathing apparatus weighed approximately 60 pounds.

The field evolutions provided me with first-hand data on what characteristics fire fighters valued in the formation of a cohesive unit, as well as with data on specific team efforts. For example, the first evolution was a barrel crawl which provided the basis for later search and rescue procedures. Face masks were taped to simulate the darkness in a smoke-filled room. Twelve barrels were placed in three rows of four each. After being spun around, each team worked its way from the first to the twelfth barrel by going up one row and down the next. Verbal and non-verbal communication was stressed so that the men would learn to be aware of their partner's activities during actual search and rescue operations.

Team effort and communication also were stressed during the second evolution which consisted of climbing the outside of a four story fire tower in full bunker gear to the roof. There, teams of two with taped face masks, entered the door and crawled down the stairs to a maze. Instructors provided various verbal and physical barriers intended to confuse the teams. Throughout the week men encouraged each other through the evolutions, encouraged each other to keep calm, develop their sense of direction as they systematically practiced their search and rescue evolutions.

On the third day the men participated in search and rescue procedures in the burn building, which was a multi-story concrete structure in which pallets and hay were burned. This situation, with the fire, smoke, intense heat and darkness was designed to build fire fighter confidence. I entered the building on two occasions to experience what fire fighters face each time they enter a structure fire. I went to the first level to experience what it was like not to be able to see, to bear the heat and to try to place confidence in the breathing apparatus. Observing the search and rescue procedures was interesting and informative, but even these activities were not distracting enough to overcome feelings of confinement and to still the thoughts of panic. I found my way out of the building after about four minutes.

During their training, the advanced fire fighters discussed the stress their jobs place on family and social life. Data collected from these conversations formed a basis for the pretest administered to them at the end of the week. The Family Life Questionnaire was administered to 18 men, and 14 completed the form. The questionnaire consisted of 53 questions, of which 7 were open ended and 46 were forced choice. The questions elicited demographic information, data on education, training, and their present job, perceived stress on family and social life, and the role of their wives and girlfriends in relation to fire fighting. The data were used to devise a research instrument for the Cows Crossing fire fighters.

In obtaining information for the research, I also gained acceptance by the men. On their test day, the class was one man short. One fire fighter said that if I would suit up, he would "buddy up" with me to do his practical test. I declined because part of the test required going through the burn building. In addition, when awards and certificates were given out, the class presented me with a "Certified Public Moron" award. This I interpreted as a sign of acceptance by the group.

At the conclusion of the observation of the formal training, I was able to talk to the Cows Crossing fire fighters on many aspects of fire fighting. They respected my limited experience at the fire college and I was more accepted by the men.

Local Training

The Cows Crossing Fire Department held drills regularly throughout the year primarily because the number of "working fires" (active fires) was too few to keep fire combat tactics fresh in the men's minds. Both volunteer and paid fire fighters participated in the drills, which took place after the Wednesday night meetings. New fire fighters were taught to use the equipment and were oriented to the procedures applicable to the types of fires which occurred in Cows Crossing. The drills were a vehicle for testing new recruits as well as a way for any fire fighter to demonstrate his ability.

The training which I attended included one burn drill, two smoke drills, one search and rescue evolution and two demonstrations of new pieces of rescue equipment. In addition to direct observations, information was reported to me about other burns, disaster drills, and a hazardous materials seminar. During the drills I stood as close as possible to the scene—either next to an engine or across the street. A photographic record was made of the training. In addition to learning about how fire fighting was handled in Cows Crossing, I observed how rookies were trained and how the volunteer and paid fire fighters interfaced.

Fire Season: October, 1978–March, 1979

The fire season in Cows Crossing lasted from approximately the first of October, 1978 to the end of March, 1979. Observations were made at 11 structure fires, 3 brush fires, 1 auto fire and 4 signal 100's, which are fires "contained on arrival."

The city had a dual alarm system. The alarm first rang at the station and all off duty and volunteer fire fighters were simultaneously "beeped in." The portable beeper each man carried alerted him to fire and rescue calls through a series of coded tones and code words. All men reported to the station for a fire call unless it was a Signal 25, a "working fire." In this case, men responded to the scene of a working fire by private vehicle. When I was not at the station, I had the use of a beeper and was able to respond 24 hours a day to the fire calls. On four occasions, fire alarms came in while I was at the station. At these times, I recorded how the men donned their bunker gear, mounted the engine and rode out of the station house. If the fire was a Signal 100 I stayed behind to observe the arrival of the volunteers and the off-duty fire fighters. If the alarm was a working fire, I followed the engines to the scene.

There was also a second alarm system called "Big Bertha," a siren that was blown on all major fires. This was a back-up system used to alert fire fighters in case their beepers malfunctioned. After the alarm was sounded, I drove to the scene and parked two blocks from the fire. The community was small and familiar to me, therefore I was able to get to the scene within three minutes of the alarm. Sometimes I arrived simultaneously with the fire engines and often before the off-duty fire fighters arrived.

After attending my first fire, the police knew who I was and what my purpose was at the fire. The police cooperated with me and at subsequent fires they escorted me to vantage points for better observation. On other occasions I stood beside one of the pumpers with the engineer who could help interpret the action. Also by standing near the engines, I could monitor conversations between officers and between officers and the station house.

Observations recorded included the time, place and focus of the action as the fire fighters progressed from the initial entry into the fire, through search and rescue procedures, to salvage and overhaul at the end of the "fire combat." Observations were made of police/fire fighter interaction and fire fighter/spectator interaction. Final notes were recorded at the station after the fire as the men cleaned the equipment and reloaded the engines. I used the hour or two to observe from the tailboard of an unused engine, by walking around the bay, by watching activities outside the station or by listening to conversations in the watch room.

The time I spent at the station was important because of the intense activity and the personal interactions I recorded. The work, the conversations and the horseplay were recorded. The integration of paid and volunteer fire fighters was noted as were the remarks made by the paid men of the volunteers. Sometimes food or coffee was served as the men told each other what they did during the fire. During these times, I observed silently because the men were too involved in their work to bother answering questions.

My note-taking activities were interesting to the men and several asked in general ways what was written on the cards. However, only three men in 15 months actually came to the tailboard to look over my shoulder. The first was Jack Brown, the assistant chief, who asked to see "just what it is you write down." The second man, Joe Smith, a key informant, came a few weeks later followed by Johnny Butter, a fearless and respected fire fighter. No attempt was made to hide what I had written nor did I stop the recording process as the men looked over my shoulder.

In retrospect, it was significant that these three individuals asked to see the field notes. The men were curious about what was being recorded, and concerned that the "truth" about fire fighting and fire fighters be presented to the outside world. Also, the men were influential among the fire fighters and there is no doubt that what they saw recorded was repeated to the other men because I sensed an increase in the men's trust as a result of these events.

The Fieldwork Situation III:
The Research Instruments

In May and June, 1979, I administered questionnaires to the paid fire fighters and to the volunteers (Appendix A), and to the wives and girlfriends of the paid men (Appendix B). The questions were developed from previous conversations with the study group, and with the instructors and students at the fire college. I designed the research instruments using guidelines published by others and with the help of another anthropologist (Cargill-Mazer, 1978; Henerson *et al.*, 1978; Niederhoffer, 1978; Oliver-Smith, personal communication).

The questionnaire given to the paid men was followed by a taped interview of each man (Appendix C). The volunteer fire fighters and the women were given only a written questionnaire. Both research instruments were administered within six weeks. The instruments were used at the close of the observation period "to extend the researcher's range of awareness, to discover inferences and to verify observations" made during the previous fourteen months (Honigman, 1976:246).

The Questionnaire: May, 1979.

In May, 1979, eighteen paid fire fighters were given the Fire Fighters' Basic Information Sheet (Appendix A). The questionnaire was composed of 52 questions, of which 3 were open-ended and 49 were forced choice. The questions were grouped by subject but were not labeled to avoid biasing the responses with my definitions for topics. The questions elicited demographic data, information on education, training in emergency rescue and fire related areas, present employment and previous fire fighting experience. The questionnaire was administered at the station in the afternoon to each of three shifts. I waited in the room to clarify questions and to verify that each question had been answered.

The volunteer fire fighters were administered the Fire Fighters' Basic Information Sheet, but with far less success than with the paid men. Of the ten volunteers, eight completed the sheet. Six men were given the questionnaire one Wednesday evening in May before the weekly meeting. The instructions were gone over with each man individually and each man voluntarily participated. Four men were mailed their questionnaires and two responded.

Although two men did not participate, enough volunteers returned the forms to make general statements about the training and experience. However, unfamiliarity with the written research instrument and its wording, created some confusion among the respondents, particularly among the older men. The completeness of their responses was poor. The data elicited from these men were not analyzed in detail. Clearly a separate questionnaire designed for volunteers needed to be constructed and administered orally to individuals to elicit more data.

Fifteen wives or girlfriends of the paid men were invited in groups of four or five to coffee parties at my home and were given the Women's Basic Information Sheet. Not all the women attended these gatherings, although all fifteen did complete the questionnaire. Four women attended the evening coffee party and two attended the morning coffee party. Therefore, three women separately were given the questionnaire which was picked up at their home the next day; two women completed the sheet individually at my home; three filled it out in their own homes while I waited and one woman mailed hers to me. The women were told there was nothing secret about the questions, but that it was hoped they would fill them out without consultation with their husbands. It is believed that only one woman correlated her answers with those her husband gave on comparable questions.

The Women's Basic Information Sheet (Appendix B) consisted of 51 questions, of which 15 were open-ended and 36 were forced choice. The purpose for the questionnaire was to solicit opinions about fire fighting from women whose role was outwardly stated as ancillary to their husbands' roles. The women were very receptive to the process and most answered the questions in detail. The questionnaire elicited demographic data, information on education, training in medical or fire related fields, home and social life, their feelings about fire fighting and the role they perceived for themselves as wives of fire fighters.

Table 2
Summary of Returns on Research Instruments*

Pre-Test Questionnaires	Possible Respondents	Actual (N)	Respondents (%)
State Fire College			
1. General Questionnaire to Basic 200 Hours Class	22	10	45%
2. Family Life Questionnaire to Smokedivers	18	14	78%
Research Instruments			
Cows Crossing Fire Department			
1. Fire Fighters' Basic Information Sheet to Paid Men	18	18	100%
2. Fire Fighters' Basic Information Sheet to Volunteers	10	8	80%
3. Women's Basic Information Sheet	15	15	100%
4. Fire Fighters' Intensive Interview	18	16	89%

*   See Appendices A, B, C.

Interview Schedule: June, 1979

In June, 1979, sixteen paid fire fighters were scheduled for individual structured interviews. Two men were not interviewed: one informant, Ron Emmet, was not formally interviewed and the fire chief avoided scheduling. The purpose of the interview was, in part, to provide the men with a vehicle for giving their opinions and to elicit data not already recorded. Three men chose to be interviewed in their homes, four men chose my home and nine preferred a separate room at the fire station. Each interview lasted between 35 minutes and two and one-half hours. The average was about one hour.

The responses were taped, and each man was assured that his participation was voluntary and that the tape would be transcribed by me and then erased. All the men agreed to the interview and on the whole were anxious to participate because the interview process provided them with the opportunity to make sure that their opinions were recorded. They seemed concerned that I be presented with an unbiased view of the relationships at the station. Their answers to my questions were frank and open.

The purpose of the interview was expressed to each respondent and the questions were direct, focusing on the areas of concern. The men were asked to discuss their interest in fire fighting and emergency rescue and why they did or did not like their present position, its rank and duties. They were asked to identify the qualities that made a good fire fighter and officer (see discussion, Chapter 6). Further, they identified specific job stress and its impact on family and social life (see discussion, Chapter 7). Since the focus of the research was on small group interactions, the majority of the questions were about problems at the station as well as the formal and informal processes used to resolve those problems (see discussion, Chapter 7). Finally, they answered questions about the role of "their women" in relation to their occupation (see discussion, Chapter 7). Table 2 summarizes the returns to each research instrument used in this study.

Analysis and Composition

The data were analyzed over a 24 month period beginning in late August, 1979. The questionnaires were tabulated first and the decision was made to exclude specific data elicited from the volunteers. A brief transcription, completed with notes taken (not verbatim), of each taped interview was completed to determine general patterns of behavior and to generate preliminary ideas. Preliminary correlations between the fire fighters' responses and those of the women were drawn to get an idea about the fire fighters' family life. All questionnaire data served to flesh out the data gathered through participant observation.

In conclusion, the fieldwork was a dynamic process from which emerged research questions, research problems, key informants, and a shift in my researcher role. Methodological problems and issues were identified and resolved during the feasibility assessment. A holistic research methodology utilizing participant observation and the personal approach in conjunction with other resources was suited to the research on the interplay of persons and events in this natural group. Further, the holistic approach enhanced the research objective which was to arrive at an ethnographic understanding of the attitudes, perceptions and behavior of the fire fighters. This methodology can be used as a model in the study of comparable human organizations or in situations in which the fieldworker is of another sex or social class than the members of the study group. The following review of the literature provides both supportive ethnographic material and a theoretical orientation for the data analysis.

3

LITERATURE REVIEW

Theoretical Orientation

The research elucidates the ritual processes which function to maintain the social solidarity found among one group of fire fighters. The supportive material below defines the theoretical concepts used to analyze the field data, and is a statement of how the present research fits into and evolves from previous work done in anthropology. The fire fighters form a small group, therefore initially I examine the social structure and the nature of small groups including the structure expressed through male sex roles, the working class prototype, and male bonding. Ritual is then explored because ritual functions to confirm the roles within the group and confirms the structure of the group. Finally, the use of ritual leads to a formation of normative communitas or cohesiveness within the group.

The fire department is one group in Cows Crossing which operates in conjunction with several other groups, or subsystems, to form the social structure of the community. Social organization, which exists within groups, is a "systematic ordering of positions and duties which defines a chain of command and makes possible the administrative integration of specialized functions" towards a goal (Firth, 1964:60). It is the expected way people behave towards each other (Lawless, 1978:50). One way people organize their behavior, or are taught how to behave, is through their membership in a small group.

This examination of the fire fighters, then, is essentially research on small group dynamics. The following principles of primary group organization are used to analyze their group structure and individual behavior: the development of an informal social organization involving patterned behavior which subsequently identifies insiders and outsiders; the development of a group code which prescribes the group's norms and values; and the development of role differentiation with different levels of status within the group (Olmsted,and Hare 1978). The fire fighters are assigned roles, however, the status they develop within these roles, and their behavior often reflect the rules of their informally derived social structure.

Some groups develop norms which they use to determine group behavior through a system of rewards and punishment. For example, the fire fighters establish norms, then use ritual as a social leveling mechanism or as a disciplinary measure to enforce those norms. When group norms operate smoothly, group cohesiveness results. Cohesiveness is determined by the satisfaction the group has for its members, including *esprit de corps,* good morale and group atmosphere and a "strong leader" system of leadership (Bonner, 1959:78).

Group boundary strength is integral to the effective functioning of any group whose " . . . boundaries (were) the principles of social organization which, like kinship or other institutions, can vary in response to differing needs for organization, adaptation and survival" (Molohan, 1979:8). One of the questions raised is, "Why do (human beings) work so diligently at constructing and defending social boundaries, as well as the identities provided by boundaries . . . (when) clearly the maintenance of human social boundaries is often very costly?" (Molohan, 1979:15). The present research attempts to answer that question by describing the job of fire fighting and its interpretation by one group of men.

The fire fighters are organized along paramilitary lines, and the paramilitary structure allows for either the development of an authoritarian leader or for the development of democratic leadership. By comparing the two types of leadership, I gained some insight into the motivation behind the informal interactions among the fire fighters. One important issue is whether paramilitary groups with a leader-centered structure are less satisfactory to group members than are groups with democratic leadership (Bonner, 1959). Authoritarian leaders stress discipline, utilize instruments of power inherent in their offices, require deference by the group of certain symbols, and rule through a fear of punishment. In groups in which leadership is shared, the group is more effective in achieving its goals, and individual levels of personal satisfaction are higher than in leader-centered groups (Bonner, 1959). An alternative to authoritarian leadership and group leadership is the development of a strong leader, a role which could easily develop in paramilitary structures. Bonner states that "people do not object to strong leadership, provided that they know that they can participate and take initiative if they want to" (1959:192).

The literature also questions the positive and negative affects of group interactions relative to group effectiveness (morale). Persons who interact frequently tend to form positive responses with reference to each other (Bonner, 1959:79). Also when groups face danger together and overcome it, the members' feelings toward each other become positive (Bonner, 1959:79). Group disruption may also be a natural result of members' interacting with each other (Bonner, 1959; Barth, 1969). There are "major disruptions," with group factions forming, a relative absence of leadership, little *esprit de corps* and the permanent withdrawal of some members; and there are "minor disruptions" with temporary interpersonal aggression and a general disorganization of the group (Bonner, 1959:88). These categorizations made it easier to analyze disruptive events and the rituals used to re-establish group solidarity.

Through an analysis of structure and leadership patterns, I compare small group studies of non-military groups to the paramilitary fire fighters. For example, in Whyte's (1955) study of street corner society, the group's social structure is based on a hierarchy of personal relations: the corner boys judge a man's capacities according to the way he acts in his personal relations. They develop a network of reciprocal obligations among themselves from which arises group cohesion. The leader is the focal point of the group because he decides group activities, arbitrates disputes between individuals and serves as confidante to the others. The formal structure of a small group, then, including its type of leadership, theoretically determines in large part the interactions between individuals within the group.

There is another ingredient which determines how men interact with each other. This is a label they use to define each other: "masculine," or "a man." Many studies deal with the concept of masculinity and with the notion of male bonding, or the idea that men like to be a part of all-male peer groups both on the job and during leisure hours (LeMasters, 1975:21). Working class people adhere to this notion and to a belief in the segregation of the sexes. Their tradition includes society's support for male dominance over women; a division of labor along sex lines; a male cult of sexual prowess coupled with an abhorrence of homosexuality; and a cult of toughness including a readiness to defend oneself, one's woman or one's buddy (Yorburg, 1974:153–180; LeMasters, 1975:92–99, 107–109).

In every human society there is a category of activity which is perceived as exclusively and predominantly male (Rosaldo, 1974:19). This notion is culturally legitimated, and its exclusivity makes the activity overwhelmingly important. Further, the role played by males has a public orientation opposite the domestic role established for women.

In the cult of sexual prowess, sexual contacts between "real men" and women are characterized by male dominance (Fasteau, 1974), and sex is a large topic of conversation with attendant "joshing" and bragging about sexuality (LeMasters, 1975:104). The cult of sexual prowess is tied to the cult of toughness in cases where men believe they have to defend "their women" or defend themselves against accusations of homosexuality.

The cult of toughness is central to the achievement of the label "masculine" and masculinity in the United States is depicted as a vague essence for which males must fight and acquire (Fasteau, 1974:16; Fein, 1977:188). The label is accorded to boys and men who "measure up" to the standards of toughness, coolness, competence and sexual ability (Fein, 1977:188).

Competitiveness and disregard for their own personal safety is reported as common means men use to attack and solve personal problems (Fasteau, 1974:15–16). In all-male groups there may be greater pressure for men to establish themselves and may pose a greater threat to their identity than for men in mixed groups (Aries, 1977:295). Competitiveness overlaps into personal relations, and within some small groups men are reportedly concerned with the position in which each stands in relation to the others (Aries, 1977:296).

A corollary to male competitiveness is the notion that males, as compared to females, remain unemotional and avoid intimacy with other males (Yorburg, 1974; Fasteau, 1974, Aries, 1977; Fein, 1977). Instead, warmth and friendship are acknowledged in the form of joking and laughter (Aries, 1977:296). Intimacy and dependence may be forced on men by the nature of such occupations as policeman, fire fighter and soldier, but these jobs have such well developed masculine images that men can behave in ways which would be suspect under other conditions (Fasteau, 1974:16; Caputo, 1977). Touching is to be avoided, although it is used by men as a gesture of dominance. Mock play between men —pushing, wrestling, lifting each other—is used to maintain a status hierarchy among friends of the same sex (Henley, and Thorne,1977:216). Despite this prohibition against intimacy many men apparently prefer the company of other men during structured work time as well as during recreational periods (Caiden, 1977:129; Niederhoffer, 1978:47 Tiger, 1969: 93–125). The image that male bonding presents is that of a team or group of "pals" or "buddies" bonded together to fight a common enemy, to help a comrade or to solve a problem (Fein, 1977:194–195). Further, male bonding generates considerable emotion and male-male interactions provide important satisfaction which males could not get from male-female interactions (Tiger, 1969:101–102). Masculinity, then, presupposes male dominance over women, toughness, sexual prowess, a preference for associating with males during work and leisure hours and an abhorrence for homosexuality.

Traditionally the military, the police and fire service have been male dominated organizations in which women serve in small numbers. Military and police studies provide rich comparisons to the fire fighters particularly with reference to the subjects of group interaction, group cohesiveness, stress and the coping mechanisms used to relieve stress.

In general, observations of military group interaction indicate that group identification increases under conditions of external danger (Janis, 1963). The primary group for a combat soldier meets his individual needs for reassurance by fostering group cohesiveness in several ways. First, men vow to help each other; use humor to relieve tension; discuss the danger before it happens in order to reduce tension; and they reassure each other that they are not "sissies" (Bourne, 1970:96).

One study of World War II Air Force Bomber teams delineates several aspects of group cohesiveness which include the following characteristics: individuals are assigned specific jobs, but recognize the need for mutual aid; officers and men in combat become concerned for each other as individuals as the stress of combat weakens the militarily imposed hierarchy; men who face combat together are considered by each other as "brother;" and the bonds made in the combat units are related to the ability to withstand stress (Grinker, 1945).

Helicopter ambulance crews (Medevac units) serving in Vietnam were located in Saigon away from immediate combat (Bourne, 1970). The stress of boredom resulting from this inactivity change when they fly in 4-man crews, under fire, to rescue the wounded in combat zones. This alternation of boredom/stress and hazardous duty/stress parallels that faced by the fire fighters.

The Medevac crews utilize effective psychological defenses which enable them to minimize the affective response to the dangers of their job. These defenses are evident when men are reluctant to discuss the dangers of their job; when they deny there is any real danger; when they view circumstances as unique if colleagues are killed; and when they emphasize the rewards of their job, such as the prestige and gratitude (Bourne, 1970:96). Stress is alleviated, in part, by their discussing close calls and by their overemphasizing the dangers in a given situation.

The results of Bourne's physical and psychological stress tests on one Green Beret unit have implications for understanding stress in a variety of paramilitary and non-military settings. Stress results from the anticipation of a strike by enemy forces and from the frustration ensuing from periods of inactivity alternating with the high stress of combat. The vacillation of different stressors again parallels those faced by the fire fighters.

While in combat, Marines in Vietnam deal with the male sex role as assigned to men by their society — toughness, masculinity, bravery, heroism and the proving of oneself. To prepare the Marines for combat, their training includes mental and physical abuse which is justified by the idea that a man who cannot take shouts and kicks during the training maneuvers will not be able to endure a combat situation (Caputo, 1977:7–12). The comradeship which develops during training and during combat helps create a cohesive functioning unit.

The police revitalization movement is trying to make the police more representative of American society (Caiden, 1977:129) by including minority groups and women in its ranks. This revitalization occurs, in response to the objectionable homogeneity of the group. Police studies also deal with the role assigned to a select group of men by their society (Caiden, 1977:131). Police work is seen by the public as men's work with the image of a police officer as a crime fighter, a frontier hero. Image is an issue of great importance to the police, who are conferred with powers by society, and yet often are treated as servants (Niederhoffer, 1978:42).

Radcliffe-Brown and Victor Turner had the greatest influence the theoretical development of this research, with their respective uses of the concepts of functionalism in anthropology, and the function of ritual processes in human groups. As is done in this research, the functional approach may be used to study the function of a social act by examining its affect upon individuals

(Radcliffe-Brown, 1952:184). I utilize Radcliffe-Brown's differentiation between historical and theoretical study by applying his two terms of logic: idiographic and nomothetic. With idiographic inquiries, a social scientist may collect factual data which are then linked to the acceptable general proposition arrived at through nomothetic inquiry. Nomothetic inquiry is used in the search for patterns, rules or norms within societies and is a technique which works well in a participant observation research methodology.

The examination of the role of ritual processes in the maintenance of social structures continues to be an important way of discovering patterns of behavior. Modern industrialization and urban civilization have produced extensive changes in social structure. There has been a decrease in the importance of sacred ceremonies as secularization increases, although, "there is no evidence that a secularized urban world has lessened the need for ritualized expression of an individual's transition from one status to another" (van Gennep, 1960:xvi). For example, the fire fighters use two minor and two major ritual processes to mark the transition of its members from one status to another, and to maintain the social solidarity of their group. Ritual processes have been recognized by many anthropologists as serving similar functions in other societies (Turner, 1968; 1969).

There is a relationship between ritual behavior and the dynamics of individual and group life (van Gennep, 1960; Chapple, 1942; Turner, 1969). The analysis of ceremonies accompanying an individual's "life crises," is van Gennep's (1960) contribution to an explanation of why ritual processes occur. The process of joining a group is described as a gradual one, marked by rituals at each stage of acceptance by the group. In these rites of passage, an individual is first separated from previous ties. This is followed by a transitional period, and finally the individual is incorporated into the group (van Gennep, 1960; Chapple, 1942). These major phases then—separation, transition, and incorporation — are the dynamics of process and structure.

Van Gennep's rites of passage provide only a general framework for explaining the function of the fire fighters' complex rituals. Their ritual ceremonies contain many variables and therefore must be considered as composites, requiring analytical input from several anthropologists. Chapple's (1942) rites of passage and rites of intensification contribute to the present analysis because he talks about the relationship between the individual and the group. Life crises (e.g., puberty) may affect only the individual and a rite of passage may be the ritual process used to help the individual attain a new status in life (e.g., adulthood). The focus of the ritual in this case is on the individual. However, life crises may cause disequilibrium within a group also affecting other peoples' relationships with the individual, and rites of intensification may be used to restore a balance to the relationships between the people within the group. The focus of the ritual in this case is on the group and its level of solidarity.

Ritual symbols are also part and parcel of the ritual process. Warner (1959) discusses an American ritual involving the participation of many groups which recognize the same symbols, such as the rituals and symbols surrounding Memorial Day. He cites twenty-one forms of secular ritual which are concerned with the internal relations of a small group in his study. These activities are created by group members and function to emphasize the unity of the group, and to maintain indirectly the feelings of the members their separateness from the larger society (Warner, 1959:237).

Rituals have observable structures, and the ethnographic literature contains many examples of marriage, funeral, puberty and curing rituals. Under the observable structure of a ritual may be detected the telic structure, which means that the "ritual conceals below it a system of social relations" (Turner, 1968:2–3). The roles involved in ritual ceremonies have connections with those roles found in other rituals and with non-ritual roles.

Ritual forms a complex system which has a symbolic structure, a value structure, a telic structure and a role structure. Further, ritual activities "appear to be purposive; even if they do not seem to be directed to the achievement of any practical results, they nevertheless have effects upon the participants which influence subsequent behavior" (Turner, 1968:6). Therefore this study uses the eight aspects of ritual which Turner identifies to help organize both people and their social experience into an order. For example, rituals of affliction or redress function to affect the behavior of the group. First, if social solidarity is the product of a ritual action, then it must be further supposed that a ritual sequence arises from some social desire for that solidarity. Second, the decision to perform a ritual is itself a mark of unity among the participants. Third, several people may agree to attend a ritual ceremony, and this agreement may arise between people who differ, but who wish to transmute their differences into authentic solidarity. Fourth, ritual is concerned with securing a balance between parts of the group. Fifth, the ritual prescribes that the individual subordinate his individuality to the social roles assigned to him. Sixth, the individual must be promised some reward for his subordination. Seventh, what is aimed at is the individual's acceptance of the social norms of the group. Finally, eighth, when each individual "is induced to act in conformity with social norms . . . the component groupings of his society will be in 'something like' the right relation" (Turner, 1968:270–271). This interesting phrase, "something like the right relation," means that the very norms of the social structure produce disputes, which create disequilibrium, and which subsequently require the application of ritual processes.

When disequilibrium occurs, a drama ensues in which both the conflict and the desired change are stated explicitly. If any group intends to restore itself to "dynamic equilibrium," it is presumed a conflict has occurred, that there is a victim, that s/he is condemned as a norm breaker and that punishment must ensue (Turner, 1968:276). An innovator may be the subject of punishment (i.e., the subject of ritual) because "the introduction of novelty would prevent the ultimate closure of the social circle" (Turner, 1968:277) and solidarity would be threatened. The victim — or norm breaker, innovator — may be the scapegoat for individual group member's feelings of frustration for a perceived loss of solidarity. Rituals of affliction do not anticipate strains and tensions within a group. However, they are designed to contain or redress them once they have begun to impair seriously the orderly functioning of group life (Turner, 1968:280).

The models and processes of liminality and communitas are developed by Turner (1969). He used van Gennep's three phases of ritual as a point of departure for his discussion of liminality or transitional phase. During the liminal phase the subject of ritual stands outside the social structure, and the spirit of communitas is most evident. Rituals of status elevation, and rituals of status reversal may occur during liminality.

Communitas appears to be a spiritual communion with one another, rather than individuals standing side by side. I prefer the more specific delineation of "normative communitas" in which, over time, there is a need to develop, mobilize, and organize resources . . . (and there develops) the necessity for social control among members of the group in pursuance of these goals . . . " (Turner, 1968:131). This describes more adequately the development of the social solidarity manifest among the fire fighters and more adequately sets the stage for the ritual dramas they use to ensure the continuity of their normative communitas.

Anthropologists do not describe rituals as being separate from the cultural or social contexts in which they operate. They realize that ritual must be examined by the declared purpose for its occurring, the conceptual categories in which these purposes are framed and in terms of the audience and participants who use these categories (Leaf, 1974:127). Rituals occur in context, not in and of themselves.

After Leaf reviews the ritual theories, he is left with two questions: "What is ritual?" and "What does it do?" I agree that to understand the function of a ritual, one must consider what is objective and obvious about ritual. First, by using his information theory, I put aside two linear models previously used by anthropologists to explain why ritual processes are used. The first models I put aside are below (Leaf, 1974:156).

Linear Models

1. society becomes unstable → ritual → social stability re-established

2. individual undergoes → ritual → new status is, in consensus,
   a change, needs   accepted
   new status

These models do not answer questions about the affect of any variation that may be introduced into a ritual, nor do they answer questions about the alteration of the message if a ritual is altered. I agree with Leaf's proposed cyclical model which does account for repetition and change in the communication patterns, or accounts for the maintenance of the communication system itself (Leaf, 1974:157). Leaf's contention that ritual processes function as message transmitters is used in the analysis of ritual among the fire fighters.

3. A General Cyclical Model in Communication

INFORMATION SOURCE
(socially organized constraints upon and resources for the
organization of communication; e.g., social stability)

TRANSMITTER
(person who is ritual leader)

RECEIVER
(person who gets message;
e.g., novice, initiate)

CHANNEL
(manner in which message is conveyed; e.g., ritual)

NOISE
(additional input into channel that confuses the transmission)

Ritual is a communication process. People attend a ritual because of their own desire for a reaffirmation of the social order. "In showing ritual as a communicative process in relation to social message sources, it opens the door to an expanded understanding of the nature of social communication itself, and, ultimately, to the way in which consensus in society . . . can exist and be forceful" (Leaf, 1974:160).

In summary, the fire fighters' rituals are divided into major and minor categories. There is some consistency in the ritual process, but the fire fighters feel free to introduce variables, such as time and symbols, in any one of the ceremonies or at any stage of the ritual process. Such behavior makes it difficult to fit their ritual processes into any one pre-existing model. Instead, different models are used to analyze different rituals. The most applicable models are van Gennep's rites of passage, Chapple's rites of intensification, Turner's rites of affliction or redress, and Leaf's overall notion that ritual processes are message transmitters. The important thing to remember is that which ever ritual process the fire fighters use, it functions either to welcome newcomers, orient them to the norms of the group, or to maintain group norms as the focal point for the group's cohesion.

The supportive material on southern communities provides a cultural context for the description of the fire fighters. The community is a combination of social units and systems performing major social functions which have locality relevance. Community values provide insight into the regional, cultural and social contexts in which the fire fighters live and work. Using a systemic analysis, a community can be delineated by a horizontal relation between subsystems to each other or by a delineation of the vertical relations of local subsystems to extra-community systems (Warren, 1972:163). For example, the fire department is a subsystem which interfaces horizontally with several law enforcement, medical and other fire subsystems both within the county and outside the county of their jurisdiction. On political and economic issues, the fire department interfaces vertically with the local government agencies. These subsystems cooperate to provide an integrated fire fighting emergency medical and disaster preparedness system.

People living close together form social structures in which these systems function to sustain life and provide satisfaction to members of the community (Warren, 1972:165). Local values are reflections of a larger culture and provide a standard by which small groups can measure themselves. Values and standards are important to the fire fighters, who use a code of ethics to measure their own and each other's worth. One community value is neighborliness, expressed through a system whereby individuals exchange work within their social classes (Arensberg and Kimball, 1965:126; 176–178). Another study identifies white community values as "privacy of the home, the sanctity of womanhood, fulfillment of obligations (especially those based on one's word), rights of property, defense of one's honor and resistance to the intruder" (Arensberg and Kimball, 1965:172).

In addition to the values found in southern communities, rural communities throughout the United States share the values of friendliness, neighborliness, support for individuals along occupation or class lines (Vidich and Bensman, 1960:34–37; Hostetler, 1968:6, 145; LeMasters, 1975:24–25). Also valued are a public ideology of equality, a respect for work, public courtesy, and support for public service institutions.

Urbanization, industrialization and bureaucratization are processes which shape the structure of the American community life and influence the functioning of the inhabitants (Stein, 1960; Killian, 1970). Local community autonomy in the establishment of goals, policies and operations of community units is giving way to increased control by extra-community influences, such as from the federal government. However, the people of many southern communities are politically conservative and believe that local autonomy and states' rights are preferable to federal intervention on any issue, and their local government and business groups slow the effects of the "great change" (Warren, 1972:94). One way to retard the effect of change in the South is to maintain old social organizations and retain social control over blacks and poor whites. The caste/class system is maintained more easily in rural areas where the effects of urbanization, with its attendant opportunities for education, employment and so forth, are reduced. Although southern regional subcultures have been disrupted by the forces of urbanization, industrialization and bureaucratization, a caste/class structure persists in the rural South at this time. Social change is altered by this "rural/urban barrier, which kept large numbers of whites as well as blacks in a low income status, (and) was more formidable than the race barrier . . . " (Killian, 1970:49).

In many southern communities the social situation does call for changes in attitudes toward outside influences, but the old social structure is powerful enough to mitigate the effects of social and economic change. In sum, the pace of social change is slowed and the cultural distinctiveness of southern life in general results from a continuing caste/class structure, a rural/urban split and a perpetuation in the rural areas of the old values of neighborliness, religious affiliation and self sufficiency. The forces for change which the residents of Cows Crossing face in the 1970's and early 1980's are discussed in the next chapter on the research site.

4

AT COWS CROSSING

Southern Communities

Cows Crossing provides the cultural and social context into which the fire department is integrated. A complete community study is not part of the present research. However, the following brief description and analysis of the community relies in part on my personal experiences in the community. During the four years I lived in Cows Crossing, I became aware of many cultural and social forces. The following is a combination of personal insight, empathy and objectivity towards the interworking of persons, events and subsystems within Cows Crossing.

Cows Crossing is a small town undergoing change, but the people retain a sense of the rural South. Cultural pluralism provides a way for Southerners to remain distinctive. Pluralism means "an effort of a group to cope with the problem of preserving its distinctive, historical identity when the demands of a national unity threatened to override subsocietal loyalties . . . (Also it) constitutes the effort of the subgroup to maintain the power to protect its own self-defined interests in a society in which the rule of the majority or of the dominant minority, denies 'minority rights'"(Killian, 1970:123). Southerners have become alienated from mainstream American society (Killian, 1970:117, 144), although the people of Cows Crossing would not use the term "alienation" to describe their relationship with the rest of the United States. However, they do refer to themselves as "different from the Yankees" and continually make reference to "how we do things here."

White southern distinctiveness is emphasized by a recognition of white Southerners as an ethnic group which: (1) is largely biologically self-perpetuating; (2) shares fundamental cultural values that are realized in overt unity in cultural forms; (3) makes up a field of communication and interaction; and (4) has a membership that identifies itself, and is identified by others as constituting a distinguishable category (Naroll, 1964:284; Killian,

1970:10). Ethnicity, then, is to a great extent dependent upon self-conscious cultural definition, self-ascription and identification (Barth, 1969:10).

Regionalism is maintained in Cows Crossing and in the South as a whole through the use of a distinctive dialect, a romanticization of the Civil War, anti-northern and anti-union feelings, a tendency to deal with problems in a violent manner, the influence of the two powerful institutions of church and family, and a unique position of having to teach history from the side of the loser (Killian, 1970:9–10, 121; Reed, 1972:45–46, 57, 86–87). Reed suggests that "in the quest for a central theme as to why the South remains distinct is the image of a people defined in opposition to a powerful, external threat" (1972:88).

The persistence of a "southern mind" is crucial to the existence of a "regional cultural" identity (Reed, 1972:ix). This is evident in Cows Crossing by the residents' tendency to select normative reference individuals from among kin and neighbors, a belief in corporal punishment of children, a belief in the right to private ownership of guns, and a belief in fundamental Protestantism (Reed, 1972:9, 45–46, 48, 57, 87). The southern mind opposes outside threats which historically have been responsible for changes in southern institutions. One way a community may deal with an unreasonable outside world is to ignore it, and to seek validation and support from the local community members (Reed, 1972:89).

One manifestation of the external threats perceived by southern communities are the forces of change brought by urbanization, industrialization and bureaucratization which have threatened to alter the way of life in the South (Stein, 1960:71). These forces bring changes in population structure, government, educational opportunities, economic advancement and changes in personal behavior. They alter, or attempt to alter, traditional social structures such as the social system founded on differentiations of caste and class.

To understand part of the life in Cows Crossing, I examined briefly its history and geographical layout; its economy and plans for the development of the community; the general community values, and its caste/class social structure. By exploring these topics, it will be evident that although forces for change do alter the traditional social structure somewhat, the Cows Crossing residents prepare themselves to slow or to control the effect of the changes by retaining their cultural distinctiveness.

At Night the Police Turn Off the 'Redlights'

Cows Crossing was originally an Indian settlement, located along the shore of a large river. In 1820 the white residents named the settlement Cows Crossing. Its pre-1884 economic well-being is attributed to winter tourists and to the cypress lumber industry.

A fire in 1884 destroyed the entire downtown except for the courthouse. The business district was rebuilt on a street perpendicular to the river making the downtown area "T" shaped: the river is the top of the "T" while the main street forms the upright portion. Downtown businesses remain on this main street as well as along the "four lane," a street one block north and parallel to the main street.

North and south of the main streets lay large residential areas with older "traditional southern" style homes. These residential areas contain many historic sites, and in the 1970's both sections were designated "historical" by the city. One of the largest and oldest mansions in the town was restored in 1978–79 as part of the River Redevelopment/Historical Society Project. It was originally built as a private residence in 1854, and was restored as such, although during the Reconstruction in 1866, the house served as a school for freed black children. South of the main street, just a block from the river, are two other historic homes. One was built by the Andrew Mellon family as a home for a male relative who was not "quite right." Across the street this man built a home for his two favorite teachers; the home now is owned by the fire chief.

Parallel to the river in the downtown section are the post office, sheriff's department and county jail, city hall, the library, the electric company, the city park and dock and a marina. Improvements on these buildings and grounds are part of the River Redevelopment Project. A new high rise apartment building is located at the point where the river and the main street meet. Moving along the main street away from the river is the Social Security Administration, the courthouse and its annex, the bus station, public health department, mental health facility, the school administration building, the fire department, city police department, the chamber of commerce, and the newspaper office. The town's services are centralized, but they serve the entire county.

Small businesses are situated between these places on the main street and along the four lane. Other residential areas and clusters of small businesses are located on the hills west of the downtown area. Outside the city limits, but still considered part of the community, are the hospital, new shopping mall and the community college.

Living in one of the downtown neighborhoods is pleasant because it is possible to walk along the river and catch a breeze all the way up the main street while shopping or conducting business. A popular "coffee-break" spot is a small restaurant which specializes in large slices of homemade pie, hefty waitresses and the morning news. The grounds around the courthouse, adjacent to this restaurants are spacious, neat and shaded by a huge water oak–the "hanging tree." The benches and gazebo/bandstand make an attractive resting place from which the Civil War Memorial can be observed.

The city is small and there is not much to do downtown after dark. At dusk, the city police turn off the redlights (stop signals) along the main street. However, the community in the county has vitality and the people are active in many events.

Of Paper Mills and Plans for the Future

Cows Crossing had a population of 9,300 in 1979 and is the county seat. For people living all over the county, it is the physical center of many activities; principally legal, but also economic and cultural. The county has a commission type of government, while the city has a city manager-commission form of government. Police protection is provided by 25 officers, a county sheriff's force of 41 and 14 State Highway Patrolmen. The fire department has 18 paid men, while other communities have all-volunteer fire departments.

The county of 803 square miles is inland, but is bisected by a large river and has a number of lakes. The county population in 1979 was 45,000 but growth is expected and the county is planning new shopping malls, hotels and apartments throughout the area. Cows Crossing is the town in which a great deal of growth is expected because of its location on the river and because it is the county seat. The downtown business district covers approximately 20 square blocks; but shopping areas extend beyond the city limits.

The economy in the county is primarily based on manufacturing and agriculture. There are seven manufacturing companies which employ nearly 3,800 people. Of the state counties having populations over 18,000, this county has the largest percentage of industrial workers. The county is also part of a large potato growing area, while other cash crops include ornamental plants and flowers, citrus trees and beef cattle. There were 441 farms in 1974 with an average value of over $77,000 each (State Stat. Abst., 1979:107). In 1975, the per capita income for the residents of Cows Crossing was $3,370 (State Stat. Abst., 1979:107). Although there is a business district in Cows Crossing, the middle class is small and the wealth of the area is controlled by a few. The majority of people are working class or lower class.

The paper mill was built in 1949 and is a major influence in the economic well-being of Cows Crossing. Although management policy precludes interference in local politics, the mill does contribute tangible items to the community. It established a memorial forest west of Cows Crossing for use by the Future Foresters of America, and a public forested sanctuary which became part of the Appalachian Trail System. During the winter, when the wind blows out of the northwest, the paper mill pollutes the town. Residents, who remember how poor they were before the mill came, merely shrug and say, "smells like money to me." Rumors about the mill, its ownership, possible layoffs and union activity are a constant source of conversation and consternation in Cows Crossing.

The financial well-being of its citizens is important to the members of the city commission and they realize that the town cannot rely solely on the paper mill for its economic growth. The commission and the chamber of commerce try to attract small industries and retirees to the area. However, the commissioners are selective because they are aware that changes in the economic structure can pave the way for extra-community influence in other areas of the community life. They want to avoid what Warren calls "great change" in local community autonomy in the establishment of goals, policies and operations (1972:52). Change and growth are welcome, but only if local autonomy is retained.

One problem in attracting industry is the appearance of the town, which looks run down. The River Redevelopment Project was conceived as one way to solve the problem. Through it, the town attracted a major hotel, replaced the bridge across the river and remounted the four bronze war memorial soldiers, refurbished the city park, renovated small residences through a federal loan program and began construction of a boardwalk and band shell along the river.

It is hoped that the large, older buildings left vacant by businesses relocating in the new shopping mall will be refurbished by lawyers and other professionals for use as their offices. The plan is a popular one, and, indeed, many lawyers and CPAs find the downtown buildings very convenient to the courthouse. The presence of the renovated buildings enhances the adjacent River Redevelopment Project as well as the nearby historic residential areas.

By taking an active role in planning for future growth, the city commission hopes to mitigate any negative effects their planned increase in urbanization, industrialization and bureaucratization may create. They think their strong feelings for states rights and for local community autonomy are powerful enough weapons to combat extra-community influences.

Community Values

Despite the low economy, Cows Crossing residents are fairly self-sufficient, a value shared by many southern communities and by rural people in other parts of the United States (Hostetler, and Huntington, 1968:18–21; Vidich and Bensman, 1960: 49–52). Except for specialized medical needs or large speciality consumer items, it is possible to buy nearly anything in Cows Crossing. When residents discuss wages or the welfare system, the phrase "taking care of your own" is repeated often. Charity is perceived as being for "the other guy."

Important to the residents of Cows Crossing are the institutions of family and religion. The more than 60 churches in the town sponsor many weekly religious observances, as well as summer revivals, camp retreats, and local missionary work. There are 319 religious organizations in the county (State Stat. Abst., 1979:457).

Community residents value the freedom to enjoy many outdoor activities. For example, there are six parades a year in which civic and fraternal groups, high school bands, law enforcement and the fire department participate. Among other events, the city sponsors the flower festival and art show and the community

college sponsors plays and concerts. Residents are able to participate in supervised recreational activities or use the facilities at
the state park (e.g., pool, community building, hiking trails, a *par
cours* trail and formal gardens). The river provides good fishing
and boating and there are nearly forty fish camps and resorts in
the area. Civic groups sponsor events on the river such as the
boat races during the winter and a sailing regatta in the late
spring. The rodeo and the county fair are held in early spring,
while fall activities include hunting in a nearby national forest.
In nearly all of these activities, families participate together.

Another important community value is public courtesy and
residents greet passers-by either with a "hey," a honk or a wave.
People are considered rude if "they do not even stop to speak."

Neighborliness is valued and people help each other with
household projects, neighbors share food (especially at the time
of a death), elderly residents are watched after and strangers in
the neighborhood are noted. Gossip is the other side of neighborliness and is regarded as a normal part of living in a rural
town. Gossip may be regarded by the residents as a way "to be
concerned about your neighbors." Cows Crossing is a community in which older ladies in cotton print dresses still make "proper" 20 minute social calls on new neighbors and sick friends.

The police department used this value of neighborliness
when it launched a "crime watch" program. By watching out for
one another and "burglar proofing" their own homes, the community residents were able to cut thefts in half in one neighborhood. The "crime watch" program also utilizes the residents'
feelings about property values and the right to defend one's
home against intruders.

Two examples are representative of the values of neighborliness and a belief in grass roots democracy combined with a belief
in the right to defend one's home. Sometimes neighbors have
different values and when clashes occur, they call a town meeting to which all concerned citizens may attend and speak.

Example #1

The Association for Retarded Citizens needed a
home for retarded males and a suitable two story older
home in an historic section was chosen. They planned
to staff the home with full time caretakers and planned
to have a small bus take the residents to a sheltered
workshop daily. The Association's director visited the

chosen neighborhood and explained the plan to each family. The residents for four square blocks were distressed at the prospect of having retarded citizens in their neighborhood, and requested a town meeting for residents, retarded citizens, their parents and the Association's staff. The owner of the home did not attend and was praised for this decision by the concerned citizens who believed that he put aside any personal economic interest for the community good. The judge also did not attend the meeting as was his custom in such cases. He did not want to influence unduly either the proceedings or his own objectivity should the process have required his legal judgment. However, it was known that the judge lived across the street from the proposed site, and that he objected to the plan "because those people howl, you know."

During the meeting several people spoke. Older female residents selected a middle aged male to express their fears for their personal safety should young retarded male citizens be allowed in their neighborhood. The sanctity of womanhood was perceived to be at stake. Landlords and homeowners spoke about their fears of a reduction in property values. They believed they had to defend their property against a future loss.

Renters were heard courteously, but were perceived by the other residents as having no commitment to the neighborhood and their opinions were disregarded. The Association argued the need for a decent place for their citizens to live, particularly after their parents died. However, they were denied the right to use the house for a home for the men. Ironically, the house was sold to a private family, who eventually converted it into a nursing home for the elderly. This was more acceptable to the neighbors who considered the nurse-owner a humanitarian who did "the Lord's work," in caring for the elderly.

Example #2

One community value changed in 1978 through an ordinance passed at a special city commission meeting. A city wide dog leash law was at issue and the meeting room was packed. Elderly residents complained they could not walk safely in the evening without being attacked by loose dogs. Ladies were "dis–gusted" (sic) at finding dog leavings on their white wicker porch furniture. In rebuttal, dog lovers extolled the virtues of a dog's running free, "like they used to with me when I was a boy; like nature meant them to." The elderly residents were successful in ridding the city of a dog problem and in changing at least the official attitude towards free running animals. The town had reaffirmed its respect for the elderly in this small way.

The community historically valued its fire department and expected it to be an effective functioning unit. The fire department has a long history of volunteerism among prominent citizens and the community expects its volunteers and the paid fire fighters to be well trained, efficient and accountable for their actions. The local press covers all fires and prints detailed accounts of specialized training held locally or at the State Fire College; it is generally supportive of the fire department. For example, when an ambulance was destroyed through an act of careless driving the public was made aware that the fire fighter/driver was disciplined according to fire department regulations. However, public support for the fire fighters as a group remains strong. The editor of the newspaper stated, "The only thing about which there seems to be no disagreement is the service provided by the men on the ambulance" (Cows Crossing Daily News, editorial, May 29, 1979).

Individual businesses provide gratuities to the fire fighters. The theatre lets fire fighters in for 25 cents if they are in uniform. The drycleaner cleans the uniforms for half price and three restaurants provide coffee or "cold drinks" free or for half price to fire fighters in uniform. These favors show support for the fire fighters, make them feel appreciated, supplement their incomes, and generally demonstrate that community residents value the men and this institution.

Blacks and Whites in Cows Crossing

Caste and class distinctions are part of everyday life in Cows Crossing. The community is racially mixed and the educational system was integrated in the 1960's. There is a public ideology of equality (Vidich and Bensman, 1960:40). The city employs blacks as workers, nurses, teachers and law enforcement officers. Blacks are farm laborers, "pulp wooders" (i.e., haul wood from the forest to the mill), and nurses' aides. However, there are no high level black public officials and they are not bankers, big businessmen or fire fighters.

Many small neighborhoods are racially integrated, but historically the town is divided into one white and one black section, the "north side." The largest section of black residences covers 70 blocks and lies north of the highway which bisects the town. In addition to residences, it contains the federal housing authority, a federal housing project, and a few small black owned businesses. On the periphery of the black neighborhood is the city maintenance yard, two ball fields, a pool, the railroad yard and a container manufacturer. The community is contained except on the eastern border where the black neighborhood blends with one historic, white residential area.

The caste/class system is maintained easily in this rural area where the effects of urbanization with its greater opportunities for education and employment are reduced (Stein, 1960). Apart from the economic position assigned to the blacks in Cows Crossing, one personal observation substantiates the effects of a caste system on individual behavior. In public, the blacks speak quietly, much more so than blacks I encountered in cities in the South or the North. Black citizens are visible everywhere, but they have "their place" and without economic or political power, they will remain "in their place" at least in Cows Crossing.

Caste/class distinctions are related directly to the economic conditions within the county. There are 907 families in the county receiving aid to dependent children, and 6,828 persons who use food stamps on a monthly basis in 1978 (State Stat. Abst., 1979:185–187). Approximately 15% of the population needs food stamps.

Cows Crossing has a welfare office, and long lines of black and white women and children are seen there on the first of each month. Both poor white and black residents on welfare are judged harshly by people from other social classes. The resentment towards the people on welfare is evident by the many remarks overheard about welfare abuses and how food stamps "are used to buy steak." Because the town is small and the welfare line extends out of the building and along the sidewalk, it is easy to observe who the welfare recipients are: that is, who the "niggers and the poor white trash are." It is not that the people of the town are against charitable giving, it is just that they resent supporting those they perceive to be "able bodied men, perfectly capable of a day's work." This negative attitude towards the poor is contrasted to the perceived plight of the "working poor" who say they manage to keep their families together without "handouts." The working class ethic of doing honest labor is a community value.

Some social scientists view the maintenance of a caste/class distinction as part of cultural pluralism, and the white Southerners of Cows Crossing are part of the oldest group of pluralists in the nation (Killian, 1970:123). Further, it is the unwritten task of many persons living in Cows Crossing to maintain segregationist attitudes, as described below.

One way the residents found to deal with an unreasonable outside world is to overrule it, or to ignore it and seek support and validation from the local community (Reed, 1972:68). This is done because the Southerners subscribe to what Killian calls the principle of concurrent majority: "a theory that unrestrained rule of the numerical majority (e.g., the federal government) would not lead to justice, but to the tyranny of the majority" over a weaker minority (e.g., state or local governments) (1970:124). Below is an example of how the caste/class system is maintained through the action taken by a city zoning committee designed to prolong a distinctive element found in many other southern communities: a consistent attempt to disenfranchise blacks.

Example #3:

During the zoning committee meeting a request to borrow $5,000 in HUD money to repaint her house was introduced for an elderly woman. Her home is in an area designated for improvement and the money was available. After the committee heard her request, the decision for approval seemed apparent. Suddenly, the chairman of the committee directed everyone's attention to "someone" in the doorway. I looked at the chairman instead of towards the door. While the others were distracted, the chairman quickly asked the housing official, "Is she black or white?" She was black and the request for the loan was denied. The decision is in direct opposition to federal mandates.

Sometimes extra-community organizations are able to force a change within the social structure of small rural southern communities. Just after the conclusion of the research period, the Southern Christian Leadership Conference approached the city and the fire department officials with an ultimatum which forced the hiring of one black male fire fighter. Apparently, black power organization activities are ongoing in Cows Crossing.

In closing, the political and social upheavals of the 1960's resulted in tokenism and continued *de facto* segregation in the South. In Cows Crossing a social structure based on caste/class distinctions is maintained despite extra-community pressure to open this closed society. Despite social change, regional distinctiveness remains in the South because of a continuing rural/urban split and a perpetuation of the old values in the rural areas. Cows Crossing provides a traditional southern cultural and social context for its citizens who value controlled economic and social growth, the work ethic, respect for the elderly, the sanctity of womanhood, public courtesy, friendliness/neighborliness, the right to defend one's property, a spirit of white supremacy and a well trained fire department.

The fire fighters use community values as a standard by which they measure themselves as a group, and each other as individuals. The next chapter presents a humanistic view of the fire fighters of Cows Crossing.

5

THE COWS CROSSING FIRE FIGHTERS

In his analysis of street corner boys, W.F. Whyte (1955) presents a very personal and human view of the young men who belong to the gang. He utilizes the personal approach to try to understand the men through those activities which can be observed and recorded. As he analyzes the gang's structure, leadership, roles, activities and goals, he describes each member as a real person and lets that person speak to the reader. Just as he deals with individuals, so the present research deals with separate humans, whose life histories are interesting and say something about why they decided to become fire fighters. Many of the men's comments below are on subjects more fully discussed later in the book. Individual's comments are presented here to describe the study group as men, rather than to discuss any particular topic. The men's names have been changed to ensure confidentiality.

Coy Conners is the 73 year old chief, and is a life-long resident of Cows Crossing. He is well respected for his position as the fire chief, for his years of service to the community, and for his success as a businessman. Under his leadership the department has changed from an all-volunteer system to a paid department with the volunteers assisting, and to a department which includes emergency rescue operations. The chief has a long standing interest in fire fighting and belonged to one of the all-volunteer neighborhood brigades before the fire department was formed. He is considered by fire fighters in neighboring communities to be a progressive chief despite his age, which is generally considered too advanced for this occupation.

The chief is part of an "old fire fighter crony" system that is carried over from his volunteer days. The older volunteer fire fighters remain part of the station life, and socialize with the paid men after the Wednesday night fire department meetings. One of Coy's favorite games is poker, and one year the men gave him a jar of quarters ($50) for his birthday in honor of this pastime.

At fires, Coy is readily visible in his white chief's helmet as he enters the fires with minimal protective gear. In the early days of fire fighting, when there were no air packs, the fire fighters merely breathed the smoke as they fought fires. The chief apparently still advocates this for himself; he is a true "smoke eater."

Table 3
Persons Who Perform Parallel Roles As Fire Fighters and EMTs or Paramedics

Fire Chief
Coy Conners (e)

Assistant Fire Chief
Jack Brown (e)

Paid Fire Fighters		Volunteer Fire Fighters
Assistant Fire Chief		Assistant Fire Chief
Jack Brown		Pete Byrd

"A" Shift	"B" Shift	"C" Shift
Captain	**Captain**	**Captain**
JW Jones (a, b, d, e)	Billy Joe Cellon (c, e)	Bob Tomlinson (d,e)
Engineer	**Engineer**	**Engineer**
Paul Jackson (e)	Sam Turner (b)	Johnny Butter (e)
Fire Fighters	**Fire Fighters**	**Fire Fighters**
Joe Smith (d, e)	Pete Johnson (d, e)	Mack Wagner (e)
Ron Emmet	Donny Small (b, e)	Tommy Lee (d, e)
Junior Turner	Brad Whitehurst (c)	Teddy Washington
		Billy Bevis (b)

(a) Officers ranked Captain or above did not run rescue
(b) Paramedics
(c) Hazardous materials instructors
(d) Members of the "committee" at varying times (see Chap. 6)
(e) Cows Crossing "natives"

The assistant chief is Jack Brown, a married man in his late 30s who has spent eleven years in the department. Under his initiative the emergency medical system was started in the county. When the county rescue system merged with the fire department, Jack was placed at the head of operations. His initiative was rewarded when the lieutenant's position was created for him so that his authority would parallel the responsibilities he had undertaken.

Jack has many of the characteristics that the fire fighters think make a good officer. He is an experienced fire fighter who has command ability. He has the administrative training necessary for a position which requires both that the department be run as a business and that it interact with other subsystems in the community. Most importantly, he is well respected for keeping his word and being honest with his men. This notion of respect is important to Jack, who said, "An officer has got to have the respect of the men. They've got to know that he knows what he's doing."

Jack is also a friend to the men as evidenced by the number of them who frequently visit his outside business office weekly. He counsels them with career and family problems and has encouraged men who wanted to leave the CCFD in search of better employment opportunities. However, when it comes to general socializing, Jack has learned to distance himself from the men. "You don't want to get on too personal a basis with them," he said. "When you have to get on someone or correct them . . . it's a whole lot worse. And it makes it harder on me . . . "

The existence of the seniority system makes it difficult for men who have grown up together to command each other. Jack experienced some initial loneliness when he was promoted to captain. "That (loneliness) got to me worse than anything else. Don, you remember Don? Well, I was promoted to captain and had a shift. Don and I lived next door to each other. He was on my shift. They were going to have a party, my shift was. At first I didn't hear anything about it. And then they were over there, then they decided, 'maybe we better go ask Jack.' Well, I don't drink, so I didn't go over anyway. Makes you think, though, 'look it here, I'm not one of the boys anymore.' From that point on, I cut off the socializing."

Jack perceives the men as family men as well as professionals, and believes the wives and families should be better integrated into the department. He advocates informal socializing for the entire department and suggested an annual picnic would be better received than the present more formal dinners. He recognizes the value of a women's auxiliary when he said, "I know I wish they were there a lot of nights to fix something to eat. Have coffee ready. Anything like this."

Most interesting is Jack's progressive attitude towards female fire fighters. He does not see any reason why a woman could not be hired at the CCFD. In fact, he feels that there is definitely a place for women generally in the fire service. However, Jack states that if he were to hire a female fire fighter, she would "not be cut any slack. She would be accorded no special privileges and would have to sleep in the barracks and would have to make her own shower arrangements with the men."

As an officer, Jack appears to be that strong leader the men want for their chief. He believes in good training, strong discipline through a system of reprimands, promotion by testing, yet empathizes with men's feelings about the rigors and horrors of their job.

One of the oldest captains is Billy Joe Cellon, who got interested in fire fighting as a child; he used to chase the fire trucks. He is a seven year veteran in the fire service, whose interest has lead him to specialized training in hazardous materials. He believes all fire fighters must have at least some minimal experience in handling chemical spills, in dealing with flammable chemicals and flameless fires and in evacuation procedures. He cites Cows Crossing as an example of a community in which the residents are not fully aware of the danger the railroad presents to them daily as it freights toxic chemicals through the center of town. He is instrumental in bringing hazardous materials training to the CCFD.

Image is also important to Billy Joe and he supports the chief in the belief that a fire fighter must perceive himself as a public servant and must maintain that image in the community. He believes individual fire fighters must be willing to give up certain constitutional rights such as free speech in public and free press in order to maintain the proper image. He believes one unacceptable opinion expressed publicly by one fire fighter would reflect negatively on the entire department. He cites the current issue of pornography as an example. Billy Joe says that "if a fire fighter was to write a letter to the newspaper editor advocating the right to read pornography, the community would believe that all fire fighters were perverts and read pornography." To Billy Joe, it is clear that community values and public image are more important than individual rights.

"J.W." Jones is a young captain in his late 20s who was promoted during the research observation period. He is a quiet, soft spoken man who does not always shout when he gives orders at the station, but who commands the respect of the others for his experience and knowledge. In his first year as an officer, he says he is distressed at the relatively inactive life he now leads. Because he has not participated in rescue operations for several months, he says he has lost his confidence in handling more complicated rescues and considers himself now better at fire fighting. When he "worked rescue" calls, he did so as a paramedic and found that job challenging, but demanding physically and emotionally. He remarked that, "It always bothered me that if you go out on a rescue call and it would be an infant; that's emotional. And it seems the older my children got, then children I rescued from that age group bothered me."

An interesting and volatile subject among the fire fighters remains the issue of unionization. "J.W." says, "I don't know that much about unions. I never worked in a union anywhere I've worked. I really couldn't say how one would work in Cows Crossing." However, by the summer of 1981, "J.W." had not only learned about unions, but joined the fire fighters union along with several men in an attempt to better their working conditions. He and two others paid their dues, but the men they convinced to join removed their support when the city threatened to fire them all. The move "J.W." started worked, however, and by June, 1981, several positive changes in hours, pay and manpower were instituted.

Another young captain in his late 20s is "Bobby T." Tomlinson, who has a life-long interest in fire fighting. As children, he and his brother "burned my father's garage down. And one time I had a plastic air plane in the garage. I took some gasoline, kerosene and mineral spirits, mixed it all together and set it afire. So my mother came outside, she put the fire out, and she set fire to my butt." Bobby T. considers himself first and foremost a fire fighter, but he feels that letting his rescue skills "get old" is not a good idea. He has thought about suggesting to the chief that "it would be best if he would let the engineer run the station for a day and let the captain run rescue two or three calls to keep your skills sharp. Because if you sit back at the station and you're not out doing it, you're gonna lose part of it."

Bobby T. takes an interest in his men, but is struggling with the problem of having to command men with whom he has grown up and gone to school. He says he needs more training in leadership, but for now his interpretation of a good leader is one who, in part, takes a brotherly interest in the men on his shift. He says, "I like to be more aware of what's bothering 'em. If a man's got trouble at home, I'd like to know about it. It's gonna stay with me—I'm not gonna discuss it with the next door neighbors. So that way I can understand how he is feeling and why he's not puttin' out his best on the job."

One of the key informants for this research, Joe Smith, –a senior fire fighter who says "I love fire fighting—there's nothing I'd rather do than go to a good working fire. It's a challenge of time, skill and knowledge." Given this attitude, it is not surprising to hear him say, "I despise rescue—ambulance. 'Lizard runs' and using us for a taxi service is the worst. Unless it's really challenging to where I know my skills are being put to good use."

Joe's ideas about the seniority system parallel the expectations he has for his own job satisfaction: he believes only those men who show initiative, skill and a "good attitude" (i.e., dedication, willingness to work) should be promoted. He believes it is dangerous to the other fire fighters to continue to use the present seniority system which promotes those men whom he believes are incapable.

Joe is generally recognized by the other men as a good and reliable fire fighter, who rarely worries about his safety on the job and who is unflappable in most situations. However, Joe says he does worry when he gets a "call out to a fight—like the other night. The person was 'supposed' to be armed, but they didn't tell us what he was armed with. Said the deputy was 'supposed' to arrive and he never did. So all the way out I wondered: 'Does he have a stick, a knife, a gun or what?' I don't like that even a little bit."

His whole life revolves around fire fighting. In addition to his regular duty, he teaches fire training classes at the vocational school and CPR classes to local civic groups. If there is a general alarm on his day off, he always responds to the fire scene. This is his job, of course, but other men have been suspected by the group at times of "not hearing the alarm" or "being out of town." Even on his days off, Joe comes to the station at least once a day to "shoot the shit with the other guys," as he puts it.

Most of the interview with Joe was spent in discussing his views of discipline and professionalism, two aspects of fire fighting which he sees as inextricably linked. And these are two aspects which he believes are lacking or are found in reduced quantities at the CCFD. In Joe's eyes officers need to be experienced and tough leaders who will mold the men into a disciplined fire fighting unit, but who will also solicit ideas from the men and give those ideas an honest evaluation.

Good officers also should issue reprimands equitably rather than as Joe maintains, "not giving them out to men who make big mistakes." The counterpart to a good officer is a fire fighter who is willing to train hard, and to work hard to gain the experience he needs to be a professional. Joe's ideas on discipline and professionalism help place him in a leadership position among the other fire fighters.

Another man in his early 20s is interested in hazardous materials training and has responded to chemical spills outside the state. Brad Whitehurst has three year's experience as a fire fighter which he gained in a station north of Cows Crossing. He says he finds his greatest joy is "knowing you're helping the community and the fact that you save human life and property. It's highly gratifying." As a nozzleman and "first in" at structure fires, his biggest complaint is about engineers who make seemingly "small errors, which means men inside a fire get burned. I have punched more than one engineer who didn't keep my water supply where it should have been," he declared.

Brad's riding partner is Pete Johnson, a Cows Crossing native and a fire fighter with three year's experience. A "riding partner" is a fire fighter's partner on ambulance runs. Unlike many of the other men who prefer fire fighting over rescue, Pete seems to enjoy the "satisfaction of helping someone in a medical emergency. Delivering a baby really makes you feel good." It might be noted here that delivering a baby increases a fire fighter's status in the eyes of the other men; Pete has delivered two.

Pete recognizes that his determination to rescue others can be both mentally and physically stressful, especially in a fire rescue situation when "you know there's two or three people inside and you work harder and may take extra risks when you really shouldn't." This tendency to take extra risks and the worry Pete says goes with it, is offset by his reminding himself "to be cool, don't get excited and remember your training."

The "fearless fire fighter" is Johnny Butter, a Cows Crossing native and a seven year veteran of the CCFD. As an engineer his most stressful moments come when "the chief's hollering for water and there isn't any." His most hazardous moments come when he has to enter a structure fire to rescue someone, but even with danger, he says he "loves fire fighting and wouldn't consider doing anything else." Johnny works hard at his job and his biggest complaint is "the 'sorry' men, who don't do their share of the work."

Bobby T. describes Johnny like this: "Johnny's not scared of nothin'. He just goes in there—he's gonna get himself hurt 'cause he don't watch overhead beams in the ceiling, he don't watch the floors. He just goes in there. All he's concentratin' on is gettin' the fire out. People like that's gonna be trouble. He's got hurt a couple of times." Despite the risks Johnny takes, he is respected for his bravery and was singled out by several men as a fire fighter they would willingly buddy up with in a fire rescue or on a charged line.

Another engineer is Paul Jackson, a Cows Crossing native who has been with the department for more than five years. In his position as engineer he feels great responsibility for the safety of the other fire fighters. He cites "tension" as his greatest physical stress on the job. In describing his job, he said, "I would say tension. The tension of a fire in the first stages. Getting things started . . . the 'check out' . . . getting your water supply started on a fire and getting your manpower in position. Once you've got your manpower at the fire and you've got water flow, and it's a good water flow, you can pretty much relax then. Knowing those men's lives are in your hands—it's a pretty tight situation for awhile."

Paul's special interest lies in fire investigation and fire prevention education, areas to which he would like to devote more time. He enjoys and believes he is best at fire investigation, "because it is like doing a crossword puzzle. Fitting all the pieces together and finding the answer. It's very exciting work." Clearly, Paul's interests lie in the more academic aspects of fire prevention.

Another conscientious engineer is Sam Turner, who has 6 years fire fighting experience both as a volunteer and as a paid man. Sam is also a paramedic. He describes himself as a innovator, and, not surprisingly, refers also to himself as an "attitude problem." He wants to reorganize the fire department from the chief down to the fire fighter level by instituting changes in activity for every rank. For example, Sam sees officers' jobs as boring and a waste of their training. He suggests, "The conservativeness of the system stops officers from being innovative. The ideal would be some sort of daily training for the officers." He believes the fire fighters also cannot get ahead because their ideas are ridiculed by the others, and because the hours the men work are so very fatiguing they are too tired to tolerate changes. His experience as a volunteer makes him understand the need for the integration of volunteer fire fighters in a paid department. He would add more men to CCFD, train them more completely and he would retire the older volunteers to honorary positions. He says his whole focus in this "structural reorganization is to improve morale." Sam's frustration with the CCFD became untenable for him and during this research he transferred to a larger fire department.

One of the most highly respected fire fighter/paramedics is Billy Bevis, a man who has come to the fire department with several year's experience in emergency medicine. He is perceived by the rookies as a thoughtful and patient man who is willing to teach the new men about rescue operations in Cows Crossing. When asked about the appropriateness of EMTs and paramedics in the fire service, Billy reasoned, "I think it has its place in the fire service because you get better quality people, physically and mentally . . . better than any person you could pick off the street and put them in a position like that because there's a lot of responsibility on both sides of it. I think your better caliber of people are firemen and I believe rescue belongs in a fire department." When Billy mentioned "better caliber of people" in his description of fire fighters, he elaborated by saying, "Anyone can be trained to do the job if they want to. The fact is whether they are physically able to do it and mentally willing to accept the responsibility of doing it. If they can do those two things, I don't see why anyone couldn't do the job." His opinions echoed those of other fire fighters who also characterize good fire fighters as capable, willing to work and dedicated to the profession of fire fighting.

An A.S. degree in emergency medicine is the goal of a fire fighter/paramedic trainee with fewer than three year's experience in the department. Tommy Lee describes his life as aimless before he became interested in fire fighting and emergency medicine as a result of a religious experience. He had prayed for "something to do to help people." After he had worked several weeks as a fire fighter, he says ". . . out of the clear blue sky it hit me that I was here doing this because this is where He wanted me to be. So I don't know if I ever became interested in fire fighting before I came here, but I asked for a certain prayer and it was answered."

Tommy likes fire fighting, but is one of a very few men who stipulated that if there were a split in functions in the department, he would "go with the rescue side . . . as bad as I hate lizard runs and everything, I couldn't stand sitting down here for 24 hours at a time just waiting on a fire." The fact that generally there were fewer than 100 fires, but several hundred rescue calls a year, gave Tommy Lee ample opportunity to practice his medical skills. The "everything" that Tommy hates includes the emotional stress brought on by "picking up little kids that have been killed. We had this one kid one night. He was a real little kid. He was 16 years old, we come to find out, but he looked 9 or 10. The kid had just gotten his first brand new bicycle and was riding out on the highway and a four-wheel drive pickup hit him. His neck was just blood and all. He was broke up all over. The biggest thing is to get there and see something like and know there's nothing you can do. Poor kid." Tommy Lee's sadness and frustration at these situations is repeated by a majority of the men.

There is only one fire fighter in Cows Crossing who says nothing about the job really bothers him. Donny Small is a paramedic with four years experience in the department, who describes himself as "cold hearted. I really can't say that anything bothers me. After you run rescue for four years, you learn to accept it [the emotional strain]. And I can't do the job if I can't accept it." When he was asked if anyone could learn to be a fire fighter, he responded negatively. "I don't think anyone can," he said. Some people aren't callous enough. Some people have feelings." Donny's attitude is atypical for the Cows Crossing fire fighters.

The last three men, Mack Wagner, Teddy Washington and Junior Turner are relatively new to the Cows Crossing Fire Department or to fire fighting in general. They range in experience from three months to three and one-half years. All three like fighting fires and believe that a combination of trust, training and experience are characteristics which make good fire fighters.

Their answers to other research questions are very middle-of-the-road. What does distinguish these men from the other men are the attitudes their wives have towards fire fighting and towards the CCFD in particular.

Junior Turner's wife is new to marriage, the community and to the fire fighting occupation. As is often the case with newly-weds, she does not believe the time she has to spend with her fire fighter is at all sufficient. However, she publicly supports her husband's career, she is trying to understand what the occupation means to their family life, and she is trying to modify her own behavior at the station so that she will be welcomed by the other men.

Teddy Washington and his wife have been married just a year and her adjustment to his long hours away from home is not complete. She seems happy that he is a fire fighter, but unlike many of the other wives, expresses no interest in learning about fire fighting or about emergency medicine. Her attitude appears to be that of an observer in her husband's career, rather than as a participant.

Mack Wagner's wife clearly states that she does not support Mack's career, nor does she see any role for wives at the fire station. She does not listen to the scanner, nor does she attend fires or fire drills. She does not discuss Mack's job with him and she states she would not join a women's auxiliary if one were formed. Her negative attitude is clear by her statement that "Risking his life every time that bell goes off . . . it's not worth his life." She also does not like to be home alone at night and urged Mack "to find an 8 to 5 job, so he can be home nights." Mack resigned from the fire department shortly after the observation period, but was retained as a volunteer fire fighter.

The Cows Crossing Fire Department is a group of like minded men who try to forge a cohesive group dedicated to meeting the demands of a dangerous job. Chapter six describes how the men create a cohesive team, and how they deal with those individuals who do not conform to the group's strict rules for behavior.

6

<hr>

CCFD FIRE FIGHTERS AND FIRE FIGHTING

The Cows Crossing Fire Department (CCFD) grew out of a long tradition of volunteer fire fighting in America. The Cows Crossing fire fighters are part of a southern cultural milieu which values self-sufficiency, honest labor, masculine men, and individual service to one's community. One of the clearest examples of public service is rendered by volunteer fire fighters.

A Sense of Tradition

Volunteer fire fighting began in Boston in 1648 when the first group was formed along with the Mutual Aid Society whose members fought fires and saved the property of members only (Ditzell, 1976:129). Benjamin Franklin organized a unit in Philadelphia in 1736. Franklin is credited with popularizing the idea of organized volunteer fire fighting in the country. The Union Fire Company was composed of 30 prominent male citizens and it served all the people in its community, not just department members. The Fellowship Fire Company was formed in Philadelphia in the mid-1700's to rival Franklin's group. The competition between these units "began a rivalry that was to characterize American volunteer fire companies" (Ditzell, 1976:31).

Many American fire companies enlisted the aid of prominent citizens. Others were formed along religious or ethnic lines, such as those in New York where companies were organized by members of the working class. The general feeling among the early fire fighters was that all able-bodied men were expected to take an active part in community affairs and fire companies provided an excellent way for citizens to demonstrate their community spirit. Up to 1850, there were no paid departments; men considered payment for service to their community as "unmanly" (Ditzell, 1976:36).

A paramilitary system within the fire department was instituted after the Revolutionary War, but took on even more military connotations after the Civil War. As an example of how these systems operated in a large city, the fire departments added "battalion commanders," "lieutenants" and departments were divided into "companies" such as engine company #82 or hook and ladder company #12. Also the paramilitary structure was introduced to maintain discipline in the fire companies, particularly in paid departments which were interested in divorcing themselves from the rowdy, competitive image of the all-volunteer companies.

Early volunteer departments were unique institutions in which the fire house was like a private club. There was camaraderie among the men who did this men's work. Women had no official role in fire fighting although they were allowed at the fire house for weekly dinners and the firemens' ball "became the social event of the season" (Ditzell, 1976:51).

In 1853 industrialization and urbanization forced New York City to organize a paid fire department which would respond to fires more quickly than a volunteer company could respond. Larger buildings required new equipment and better training for the men, and fire fighting became a full time occupation in urban areas. However, paid departments were less common in rural areas. With the advent of paid departments in the cities, the rooms above the fire houses became bunk rooms and eating areas. The fire house became less and less a focal point for social events, and increasingly became more politicized along ethnic and class lines. Paid departments remain less common in rural areas and,in the United States in 1978, 75% of the fire departments were volunteer. With this emphasis on volunteerism, it has remained a tradition for fire departments to participate in public functions. This is an expression of pride in the company and is a way to receive public support and approval.

Another aspect of early fire departments was the parochialism among fire chiefs, who believed the old ways were the best ways to fight fires. This conservative attitude covered a range of subjects from how the men were organized, what kind of uniform was worn to the nature of the equipment used and the fire ground tactics which were employed. Every advance made in the fire service was promoted with great difficulty. This conservative attitude is evident in Cows Crossing and is one point of frustration for several of the fire fighters.

Volunteer Fire Fighting in Cows Crossing

The Cows Crossing Fire Department developed in four stages. Initially there were volunteer hose brigades and bucket brigades which protected individual neighborhoods. In 1914 they formed one department. The volunteer fire fighters during these two stages were prominent citizens active in local business and government. During the third stage which began in the 1940's, fulltime men were hired to supplement the fire fighting handled by the volunteers. The paid men were responsible for getting the equipment to the fire scene, but the volunteers remained responsible for fire fighting. In the fourth stage, 1973, the city built a new fire station which housed the city fire department and the county emergency rescue services.

There was a shift in roles at this time: the paid fire fighters assumed primary responsibility for fire fighting while the volunteers assisted. The Cows Crossing fire fighters who participated in the present research are the first generation of fulltime paid men who assume the roles of both fire fighters and emergency rescue personnel and who are the first response units called in natural and man-made disasters. Although the men function in a dual capacity, they perceive themselves first as fire fighters, then as emergency rescue personnel. This perception may have been enhanced by the fact that the Emergency Medical System in the state is quite new; it began in 1975.

The Fire Department as One Community Sub-System

The CCFD cooperates with three other subsystems –law enforcement, health care delivery and volunteer fire departments–to provide several direct services: (1) fire suppression, (2) fire prevention education and code enforcement, and (3) emergency rescue and disaster preparedness in a horizontal relation of subsystems (Warren, 1972:163). The law enforcement subsystem provides the fire fighters with police protection when the men function as EMTs or paramedics in family crisis situations (family violence) or in public brawls. The police also clear disaster areas so that fire fighters have room to work. Police protection is necessary in situations where the fire fighters are prevented from doing their job because of threats from onlookers. In order to achieve a coordinated emergency health care system, hospital nurses, fire fighters and law enforcement officers attend classes on disaster preparedness and emergency medicine.

When fire fighters function as EMTs or paramedics, they assume authority and responsibility for patient care in the field. Law enforcement officials and bystanders follow the instructions of the emergency workers. After the patient reaches the hospital emergency room, authority and responsibility are transferred to the hospital staff. While transporting patients to health facilities outside the community, responsibility for their care is shared by both the fire fighters and the community hospital through the office of the emergency room physician.

Each fire department in the county, whether paid or volunteer, is assigned to a district, which is usually the city limits or township boundary. Areas in between are usually protected by the state or national forestry service. If a fire is too large or complicated for one department to handle, a call for "mutual aid" is sent out. When "mutual aid," which is aid given by fire departments in other fire districts, is rendered to the CCFD by other fire departments, command at the fire scene is maintained by the CCFD officers. The reverse is true if the CCFD renders aid to one of the all-volunteer departments in the county.

Table 4 schematically represents those relationships which revolve around crisis situations. The health care system in the CCFD county is composed of several parts: emergency rescue, emergency room, mental health and community nursing homes. When the fire fighters function within their role as emergency workers in the field, they expect to receive the cooperation of allied health professionals by radio and do not expect to receive on the scene help. The only exception would be during a large disaster when health workers may have to leave the hospital or in individual cases when a nurse or doctor stops at a scene to render aid. In a "mutual aid" situation, the assistance fire fighters receive is on the scene, and subsystems which are asked for aid are expected to provide it as quickly as possible. Simplistically, the manner in which this process relates to a victim is that during a medical emergency, aid is brought to the victim who is transported to another system for more aid, while during a fire emergency the aid is brought to the victim by one or several agencies simultaneously.

The Structure of the CCFD

The Cows Crossing fire fighters are organized in a paramilitary pattern; there are similarities between the demands placed on soldiers in battle and fire fighters on the job. Individuals in

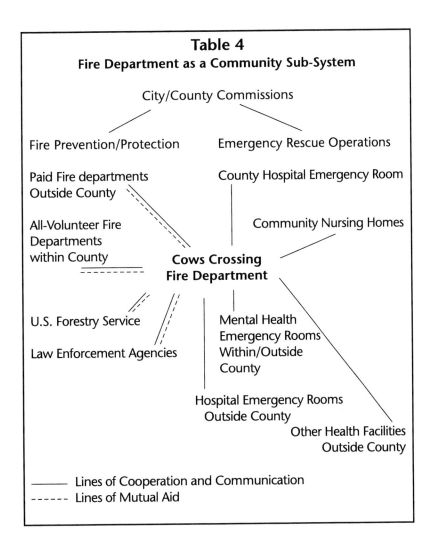

Table 4
Fire Department as a Community Sub-System

City/County Commissions

Fire Prevention/Protection   Emergency Rescue Operations

Paid Fire departments   County Hospital Emergency Room
Outside County

All-Volunteer Fire   Community Nursing Homes
Departments
within County   **Cows Crossing**
Fire Department

U.S. Forestry Service   Mental Health
     Emergency Rooms
Law Enforcement Agencies   Within/Outside
     County

Hospital Emergency Rooms
Outside County
     Other Health Facilities
     Outside County

———— Lines of Cooperation and Communication
- - - - - Lines of Mutual Aid

both groups are called upon to be disciplined, skillful, to use personal initiative and to work as a team. Survival for soldiers and for fire fighters depends on these attributes. Both groups receive rigorous training, physical screening and continuous on-the-job training. The language of fire fighting is the language of battle: officer, attack, charged lines, fireground, battalion commander, companies, alert status, watchroom, and command ability are representative terms. The disciplined performance of duty for both groups is enhanced by an organizational structure which has a clearly defined ranking system for individuals, and has attendant uniforms and badges for those ranks. Inherent in the ranking system of both groups is supposed to be the notion of pride of uniform and pride of service to one's country and one's community. The military also has a formalized ritual of respectful greeting and parting, called a salute, which is lacking in the CCFD, but which may be part of other fire departments. The military has substantially more control over the daily activities of its members than does the fire service. However, in Cows Crossing the paramilitary structure does allow the fire chief to exercise some control over the men's lives both on duty and off duty. Fire departments, then, with their paramilitary structures, have some of the attributes of military organizations. However, the degree of "militariness" varies from fire department to fire department depending on the firmness of the leadership.

The CCFD has a paramilitary structure which developed out of the previous all-volunteer system. It includes paid and volunteer fire fighters and is supported by both the city and the county commissions. The intragroup dynamics at the fire station largely revolve around the actions of three persons whose expectations for their own roles in the department conflict with the expectations by others for those roles (Table 5).

The Fire Chief

The fire chief, Coy, was appointed by the city commissioners seven years ago and will leave the job only if he retires or loses his appointment through an act by the commissioners. He works an eight hour shift and is administrator of fire personnel, director of training, commander at fire scenes and coordinator of fire prevention/education programs. He has been with the fire fighting system for more than 30 years and was part of one of the neighborhood fire brigades. He interprets his role as fire chief in a paternalistic manner. He is empowered by the commissioners to hire and fire all fire fighters. When a position opens in the department, the chief does not advertise publicly for a fire fighter. He asks the men for their recommendations or he informally approaches, or is approached by, eligible individuals in the community. After this initial inquiry, a man comes to the station to talk to the chief and fill out a city job application form. The decision is the chief's, who merely informs the city payroll about a new employee. Although there is a written guideline for repri-

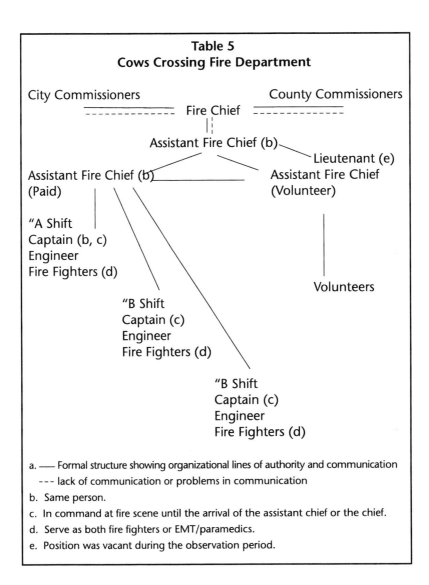

Table 5
Cows Crossing Fire Department

a. —— Formal structure showing organizational lines of authority and communication
   --- lack of communication or problems in communication
b. Same person.
c. In command at fire scene until the arrival of the assistant chief or the chief.
d. Serve as both fire fighters or EMT/paramedics.
e. Position was vacant during the observation period.

mands and dismissals, firing is handled just as informally, with the chief deciding to overlook errors or deciding to make a example of someone. No one was fired during the observation period.

The chief is the official link between the station and the city and county commissions. However, when he attends commission meetings, he goes with the assistant chief, Jack Brown, who is the real link between the two subsystems. He has better rapport with the local government agencies than does the chief, who often finds himself in an adversarial position with regard to local government by not complying with policies and procedures. Apart from any personal rivalries that may exist between the chief and certain local officials, I observed that the chief is confused about policies and procedures laid out by the commissions relative to the fire department. His confusion does not clear the channels of communication between the subsystems, and the assistant chief often has to try to change the chief's mind on various issues. Just as often, however, the chief remains unmoved and the assistant chief's efforts to keep channels of communication open are frustrated.

The greatest problem involving the chief appears to be his paternalistic interpretation of his role, which conflicts with the role as it is perceived by the assistant fire chief and by the fire fighters. This conflict in interpretation is a focal point for much of the fire fighters' frustrations. As he sees it, the fire department is "his baby," and the fire fighters' baseball tee shirts say "Coy's boys." He is an autocratic man who believes in the family, who "backs his boys" in a fight with an outside agency, but who handles intradepartmental matters arbitrarily. His arbitrariness is evident in at least three instances which conflict with the expectations held by the men: (1) the issue of pay raises, (2) the issue of a fire fighters' union, and (3) the issue of the fire fighters' civil rights.

First, the men's salaries are low and they have tried in two ways to rectify the problem. Initially, they waited for the chief to win salary arguments with the commissions, principally with the city mayor. The mayor is perceived by the fire fighters as "down on the fire department." When he voted a pay raise lower than they wanted, the chief ordered the men to boycott the drug stores in town which are co-owned by the mayor. When the chief saw one fire fighter coming out of one of these drug stores, the fire fighter reported that he "chewed my ass out."

Second, in the summer of 1978, the men talked about joining the fire fighters' union in an attempt to force the city to increase their pay. Emotions are high on the issue of unionization and the men's political feelings about unions are usually negative. However, they perceived their situation as serious enough to try unionizing. The chief heard about the meeting and reportedly "laid down the law": he said that if they unionized, their wives would no longer be allowed at the station, they would have a very structured work day and there would be only one hour for dinner. The men decided not to join the union because they would lose these privileges and because they believe they would lose local control over their station. The chief's attitudes also reinforced the men's latent anti-union feelings. The fire fighters report a negative opinion of a fire fighters' union: 69% disagree with the idea of unionizing. In the state public servants are forbidden to strike by law. Therefore the men believe a fire fighters' union is powerless. One of the experienced fire fighters, and a Vietnam veteran, Billy Bevis summed up the men's feelings by saying:

> What good would a union do a fire fighter? He's supposedly chosen his life's work because he likes it and sworn an allegiance to helping people. You can't help someone if you're standing out there on a picket line. You don't have the right to strike at a job like this.

From a personal standpoint, Tommy Lee thought a fire fighter's union would destroy the privileges he enjoys:

> The chief's good to us down here. If you needed an hour off to go to your sister's graduation or something, you go ahead and take the time off and won't get docked for it. If you need 20 minutes to run down to the bank and sign some papers, he says to go right ahead. If you're five or 10 minutes late for work, there's nothing said. Things like that. We got it good. Who wants to see it screwed up?

The chief has little to worry about the men's joining a union.

Third, the fire fighters' civil rights are abridged by the chief because he prevents them from expressing their opinions on fire and non-fire related issues through the newspaper or at public meetings. Even if a fire fighter wants to exercise his citizenship and write a letter to the editor, on any issue, that letter has to be approved by the chief. If, as with a local issue of pornography, the chief disagrees with a fire fighter's position, the fire fighter's job is jeopardized if he writes a letter to the editor. There is a status conflict for the fire fighters whose rights and duties as citizens conflict with the chief's interpretation of their rights and duties as fire fighters.

On fire related issues, fire fighters are not allowed to represent themselves at public meetings unless they have special permission from the chief. This restriction may be to ensure that CCFD presents a united public front, or that there is only one spokesperson for the fire department. However, when the chief does want the men at a public meeting, he assures them that, "any man can say anything without fear of reprimand." Clearly the men are locked into a situation in which they have little recourse but to rely on the chief's good will in order to retain their jobs.

The chief is supposed to be the director of his department and he believes himself to be just that. However, the fire fighters perceive him as "powerless" in the face of administrative problems. Further, Joe Smith says the chief "has outlived his usefulness as an officer." Others say he is too old and is not "up-to-date" in fire technology.

The characteristics of a good officer which the men outlined include the respect and trust of the men, especially at a fire scene. This respect for the chief is gone partly because of his conduct at fires. He was observed entering a structure fire without his breathing apparatus. Sometimes the men, who are dressed in full bunker gear, turn from their fire fighting to see the chief standing beside them. Many men agree with Joe's concern that, "we're gonna have to pull chief out of there one day; he's gonna have a heart attack in there."

Among the other characteristics listed for a good officer are: "good disciplinarian," "respect for the men," and "treats men equally." One of the greatest sources of frustration for the fire fighters is the arbitrary manner in which the chief disciplines and promotes them. The department has a seniority system left over from the all-volunteer system. The lieutenant's position is vacant and two captain's positions became available during the observation period. From past experience, the men expected the three positions to be filled by a move up in seniority. However, individual fire fighting and leadership abilities among the officer-candidates differed and the respect each incurred from the others varied widely. Some of the men up for promotion were considered unqualified by the man, and the fire fighters complained to the assistant chief. Therefore, a test was administered to the officer-candidates, but when none of the men passed the test, the chief promoted the senior man anyway. In a similar situation, the chief promoted a junior man to engineer over a senior man.

Fifty-six percent of the full time fire fighters responding to a questionnaire think men with seniority should have first choice only at vacations, bunk beds and TV shows. They believe promotion by testing is the only fair way to advance in rank. Thirty-one percent of the respondents simply want some consistent system by which only the qualified men would be promoted. All of the officers agree the system of promotion needs revamping or replacement.

The chief also issues reprimands which are considered by 68% of the fire fighters as necessary in any organization in order to maintain good discipline. However, 44% believe the reprimand system is not administered equitably. The men equate a "disciplined fire department" with a "professional fire department." Jack Brown, the assistant chief, says, "reprimands for petty things are given out at the whim of the chief, or are given out because he lost his temper."

The men believe that big mistakes are not reprimanded severely enough unless the fire fighter himself requests, as did Joe Smith, that the chief "follow the book on this one."

Joe is a senior fire fighter and a leader among the men. He also enjoys the reputation as being one of the fastest ambulance drivers in the department. Sam joked, "The most hazardous part of this job is riding rescue with Joe Smith!" In early March, 1979, Joe and Ron Emmet were en route to a heart call just outside the city limits. As they neared a particularly dangerous corner, Joe neglected to brake and took the corner "in excess of 60 miles per hour." As he turned, the back right tire hit the shoulder, putting the ambulance into a slide, then flipped it three times. Inside, Ron was protected by his seat belt and on the second flip caught Joe as he was heading out the passenger side window. Apart from sore muscles, bruises and a few cuts the men were unhurt. The ambulance, however, was totaled and the equipment and supplies inside were either broken or damaged.

There was a great deal of concern on the part of the men over the reaction of the chief, who was expected by several "to chew ass and chew ass." All the men were also concerned about the reaction of the commissioners and the community at large, who knew the fire chief had just ordered a modular rescue unit, the Jaws of Life rescue tool, and who had recently requested a pay increase for the fire fighters.

Joe was concerned about the men's reactions to his behavior also. Therefore, he requested the chief reprimand him as an example to the others. The chief gave Joe a written reprimand and

30 days of suspension without pay. However, the station was short one man and overworked, so Joe requested he be allowed to continue to work for 14 days without pay. The chief agreed, Joe was content that any possible animosity towards him by the others would be reduced and, surprisingly, there was no public outcry at this loss of equipment.

Clearly, the men are led by a man whom they perceive to be a "great guy," but who has lost their respect as an effective officer. There is a status conflict in which the chief is respected as a person but not as a fire fighter or as a leader. The clear hope of the men is that the chief will retire and be replaced by the assistant chief who is well respected as a good officer and whom they consider to be a strong leader.

The Assistant Fire Chief: "The Ass Chief"

The assistant chief, Jack Brown, assumed his role in 1977 after serving as a fire fighter for 11 years. The chief told Jack that he would be head of the department within two years because the chief planned to retire. This has not happened. He is a paid officer who carries out many administrative and training duties for all the fire fighters as well as commanding one shift. He came up through the ranks, but by his own initiative had assumed greater responsibilities with each succeeding year. The lieutenant's position was created for him in 1973 so that he would have the authority to direct the developing emergency medical system (EMS) for the county.

In addition to his other duties, he commands the rescue operations, assumes command at fires when the chief is not there and represents the men's interests to the chief. His administrative functions are the most time consuming and the most frustrating because he is unable to effect the changes he believes are necessary. He agrees that the standby system is grueling, although "it's not some of the things you see [at a rescue] . . . it's just that it's constant. [With] the hours that you put in, you get physically worn down. That's what it is." He thinks that if more men were hired, the standby system would be eliminated. Jack also believes the seniority system needs to be replaced by testing only. Further, he believes the reprimand system needs revamping, although he agrees with the men that reprimands are necessary to correct problems, "if a man's done something [wrong]. Not petty things, not just because you lose your temper. That's what a lot of them are."

Jack's position with regard to the volunteer fire fighters is ambiguous. As the paid assistant chief, he assumes authority over the volunteers at a fire, but training is supposed to be in the hands of the assistant chief for volunteers. The dichotomy in age and experience and training between the paid men and the volunteers made it difficult to wholly integrate all of the fire fighters. Jack believes that volunteers are a necessary part of fire fighting. However, what he wants is a "revamping of the whole volunteer system. Most of the older men are no longer qualified fire fighters and that [division] has stagnated. What we need is a well trained group of volunteers." It is difficult for the assistant chief to make any changes in this division because so many of the older volunteers are the chief's cronies and the latter's social network system is strong.

Jack disagrees with some of the men's thoughts that a union might work at the station. He thinks the best way to get what they want is to utilize the social and political networks which already exist in the community. He grew up in Cows Crossing and believes that,

> in a small, rural department like we've got, the commissioners know each fire fighter . . . if you want to talk to one of them, you can go talk to him. There's been problems in communication, but that's not the fault of the commissioners or the men. If the fire fighters have a good chief, or a good leader, he can get just about anything a department needs.

His view of the role of a fire chief conflicts with that presented by the present chief, but coincides with what the fire fighters want.

Changes are made very slowly at the station. The men take their complaints, ideas and suggestions for departmental improvements to the assistant chief and he eventually takes them to the chief. However, he says he must "wait for days until the chief is in a good mood" to ensure a positive response. Further, when both the chief and the assistant chief attend commission meetings, the assistant chief lately learned not to clarify Coy's statements as he had been doing. Jack wants the commissioners to recognize that he is not the "chief's boy" and that his ideas differ from the chief's. The result is that the men's ideas are not represented adequately to the local government because the assistant chief is not free to make public statements which may oppose those of the chief.

The dilemma Jack Brown faces is his being an ambitious man who has progressive ideas for the fire department, but who is a middleman between the fire fighters and the chief. This predicament became untenable and in May, 1979, the assistant chief took a six month leave of absence. By summer of 1981, Jack had not returned to the station and had no plans to do so.

One Key Informant: Joe Smith

The third person who unofficially has the most to say about what goes on at the station is Joe Smith, a senior fire fighter with seven years experience both as a volunteer and as a paid man. He is perceived by the others as a dedicated professional who is willing to work and who is technically capable in his job. He is considered a good fire fighter: 38% of the others prefer to have him on a charged line with them and 63% indicate they would want him to help with a fire rescue. Although many men say they would enter a structure fire to save a brother fire fighter, this man is perceived as the most likely to do so.

In his role as a senior fire fighter, he is the informal leader among the men and directs the actions of a small clique of about five senior fire fighters. They form the "Committee" and have developed, or at least enforce, a group code of ethics in their concern for maintaining discipline at the station. The Committee is concerned with the fire fighters' professional image in the community, with group cohesion, and is interested in keeping good fire fighters who are well disciplined. The Committee and this man's role as a leader developed in response to a perceived loss of strong leadership among the officers. In attempting to maintain discipline and a good fire fighter image, the key informant and the Committee try to fill a void in the organizational structure. They are trying to meet their own expectations for effective and strong leadership.

The Fire Fighters

The fire fighters of Cows Crossing primarily identify themselves and are identified by others as white Southerners, without regard for their place of birth. They share many southern regional values expressed elsewhere as community values. The men are white southern ethnics, but as fire fighters they are more accurately labeled a subcultural group (see example of Hells Angels in Molohan, 1979). Fire fighters refer to themselves as "a breed apart," or "a special breed of men."

The term "ethnic" as defined by Novak (1971:17) corresponds with the fire fighters' perception of themselves as lower-middle class, blue collar workers. Ethnic/class values include patriotism, family loyalty, anti-elitism, honest labor and neighborhood strength. Further, they are male members of the working class, a designation which brings with it a specific set of behavioral expectations. For example, the fire fighters repeatedly state it is important for a man to "know how a man's supposed to act." This vague essence, called masculinity, includes male dominance over women, a division of labor along sex lines, a male cult of toughness, a male cult of sexual prowess and an abhorrence of homosexuality (Yorburg, 1974; Fein, 1977:188).

Sexual remarks, jokes and innuendos are common at the station. For example tee shirts with sexual slogans are very popular: "Firemen are always in heat," or "Firemen have longer hoses," and "Happiness is sliding down a fireman's pole." The quickest way to start a fight at the fire station is to suggest seriously that a man is a "queer" or is sexually inadequate. Remarks are supposed to be made to "agitate" a reaction, but are made carefully enough to avoid a physical confrontation (Blanchette, 1978). However, men who are threatened by suggestions of homosexuality are prepared to fight. While there have been no physical fights at the station, there have been instances where a man "bowed up," a stance in which a man arches his back, puffs up his chest, throws his shoulders back, with fists clenched and "got right" or "broke bad" by making verbal or postural counterthreats.

Eighty-three percent of the fire fighters carry knives of varying lengths for use in their fire and rescue work. They value their personal weaponry and the right to defend themselves. Sixty-one percent of the men own guns, some of which are used in hunting while others are carried in their vehicles for protection. Carrying a weapon is part of how the men define their masculine image or their "Southerness."

Masculinity is a measure of coolness, toughness and competence. An incompetent fire fighter is considered by the others as unable to "do a man's job." He might become frightened while fighting a fire and endanger himself or other fire fighters. Such a man is called a "pussy" to his face—a label which sticks with some men for years. Brad Whitehurst is experienced in handling hazardous materials incidents. He pointed out that a good fire fighter knows how "to keep his head about him, doesn't panic and thinks before he acts." Johnny Butter is a senior fire fighter who is considered by several others as "strong as a bull and completely fearless" while fighting a fire. He is respected for his bravery, but is recognized also for his occasional foolhardiness. He is not considered the best fire fighter because he does not always think through the fire situation. However, he has never been considered anything less than "a man."

Part of this masculine image is the notion that a man must support his family. Such self-sufficiency is a value held by the community at large as well. The men report having skills other than those they learn as fire fighters. Sixty-one percent name skills such as carpentry, mechanics, surveying, electronics and welding. Half the men report having second jobs, although the standby system precludes their involvement in a regular work schedule. Some are truck drivers, welders, CPR instructors, EMT instructors, businessmen or fire science instructors on their "off days." Many of these second jobs are worked into the hours they have away from the station; 77% work fewer than 20 hours per week on these second jobs.

Job sharing along class lines is common among rural people and members of the working class (Arensberg and Kimball, 1965:117, Mochon, 1974:54). This is true among the fire fighters who often help each other in house moves, vehicle repair or exchanging other work favors. These practices are neighborly, and are often an economic necessity for a group of people who can ill-afford to hire skilled laborers for jobs around their homes. Teamwork is part of daily life, not just on the job, and working together away from the fire station also helps solidify the cohesive structure at the fire station.

Their recreational activities reflect a community wide love for outdoor sports. Two common pastimes are "mud slingin'" (or "mud boggin'") and "4-wheelin'." Both activities require a four-wheel drive vehicle such as a jeep or pickup truck; 67% have four-wheel drive vehicles. Mud slingin' means going to a boggy area and driving through it as quickly as possible without getting stuck. The drive is prefaced by bragging about the vehicle's ability, the driver's ability, setting a bet, and arranging for someone to stand by to pull the stuck vehicles out of the bog. Hubs are locked, engines revved, the vehicle is shoved into first gear, the clutch popped and the vehicle is driven headlong into the bog.

Whether or not the vehicle gets "bogged," the after effect is a lot of mud on the sides and top of the truck, and a lot of laughter.

"Four-wheelin'" is similar to mud slinging, except the driving is done in a sand pit—one preferably with hills, turns, ruts and ridges. Both activities are a test of the driver as well as of the vehicle. Usually mud slingin' and 4-wheelin' are engaged in by new owners of four wheel drive vehicles, but a number of the fire fighters have participated on a regular basis at one point in their lives.

Fire fighters, then, are supposed to be tough, sexually proficient and self-sufficient men who are technically competent on the job. These working class attitudes and the nature of the fire fighters' training have a direct bearing on the men's self image and on their behavior patterns within the paramilitary structure at the CCFD

There are eighteen men at the fire station who completed a written questionnaire which elicited personal data as well as data on education and training. The men's ages range from 20–38, with the average age of 26. The job of fire fighting in Cows Crossing is relegated to younger men.

Eighty-three percent of the men are married and 56% were raised in Cows Crossing. The rest were raised in the other parts of the state. The men prefer the South: 55% liked working in the rural South while 67% said they thought they would like working in a southern urban station. Those who like smaller towns said they "would get to know people better" and prefer smaller stations where they would be able to advance in rank more quickly. Those who chose the urban South cited "more fires" as their reason. If given the opportunity to work somewhere other than the CCFD, 89% indicate they want a paid fire station and 67% like working in fire stations with fewer than 60 people.

Fire fighters say, "fire fighting gets in your blood." Fifty-five percent of the men had been volunteer fire fighters before coming to the CCFD. Of those, 44% served in volunteer departments between one and four years. Another saying is, "fire fighters breed fire fighters." The Cows Crossing fire fighters are related to persons who had been or are fire fighters: brothers, uncles, fathers, grandfathers, sisters and cousins.

Interest in the job of fire fighting for most of the men grew over time. Some men were just looking for a job, others watched men fight fires or respond to an emergency and became interested as a result. Many had an interest which stemmed from childhood, such as the story of one young captain.The story is anecdotal, but typifies many men's interest. "Bobby T." Tomlinson says he:

> used to go down to the hobby store and buy me a model car. It'd take me three or four months to put it together, then I'd take it outside and burn it. I loved to watch it burning. My mother thought I was gonna grow up to be a (sic) arsonist. Course I'd burn the models and then put them out, burn 'em and put 'em out. Just loved puttin' the fire out. So I decided maybe I should be a fire fighter.

Of the eighteen respondents, eight men (44%) are fire fighter/ EMTs, two (11%) are fire fighter/paramedics, three (17%) are engineers, three (17%) are captains (a fourth resigned during the early stages of the research), and one is the assistant chief (Table 5). The lieutenant's position is vacant, and the fire chief chose not to complete the questionnaire.

Within the study group there is a range of years the men have been at the CCFD and the total number of years they have been fire fighters, both paid and volunteer. The seniority system promotes to officer rank those who have been at the station the longest.

Characteristics of a good fire fighter. The CCFD wants good fire fighters and the men have precise notions of what they consider to be the characteristics of a good fire fighter (Table 7). In addition to a willingness to help others, the study group believes a good fire fighter is an experienced man who is dedicated to his job and has proper training. A fire fighter and his partner should know each other's limitations and should trust each other implicitly in hazardous situations. For example, a charged line becomes a lethal instrument to the nozzleman if his partner does not maintain a support position behind him. The nozzleman is the first man in a two-man hose team. Fifty-six percent of the fire fighters want an experienced man behind them on a charged line, while 31.2% wanted someone they could trust.

Or, a man left alone to search for a victim in a structure fire runs a greater risk of losing his own life if his partner "deserts him." Therefore, 62.5% of the respondents want an experienced and trusted man as a partner in a fire rescue. The word "trust" is used frequently by the fire fighters, both when considering a man's worth as a person or as a fire fighter. In their minds "experience" and "trust" are linked characteristics. Sixty-two and one half percent of the fire fighters say they are able to trust a man at a fire after they have worked with him (Table 7). Joe Smith simply believes that "after you go with a man [into a fire] enough, you know who you can trust." The men believe that all fire fighters have a breaking point and in an assessment of any individual's trustworthiness it is important to know where that point is. The CCFD is small and men are asked to do one of several tasks at a fire scene, therefore it is important that the fire fighters be able to trust each other.

Table 7	
Qualities of a Good Fire Fighter	
Interview Questions	Times Chosen (%)
2. Qualities of a good fire fighter?	
a. Willingness to help others	37.5%
b. Dedication to fire fighting	25.0%
c. Work hard; do one's share	12.5%
d. Training	18.7%
e. Interest in more than a job; professionalism	6.2%
4. Who would you want behind you on a charged line?	
a. An experienced man	56.2%
b. Someone I can trust	31.2%
c. Anyone at the station	12.5%
5. Who would you work with in a fire rescue?	
a. Someone I can trust, experienced	62.5%
b. Anyone at the station	31.2%
c. Not very many people	6.2%
3. When can you trust a man at a fire?	
a. Work with him	62.5%
b. Know his previous experience	6.2%
c. Don't know, didn't answer	31.2%

Liking the job of fire fighting is important to the men and all of them like fighting fire more than running rescue (Table 8). Additionally, 63% of the men think they are better at fire fighting than at emergency rescue. This is interesting because the CCFD runs far more rescue calls than fire calls each week, and it seems logical that out of sheer repetition they might consider themselves better at the rescue calls. However, their interest in

---

Table 8
Job Preference

Interview Questions	Times Chosen (%)
6. Do you like your job as a fire fighter?	
a. yes	100%
b. no	0%
24. Do you like running rescue?	
a. yes	68%
b. no	13%
c. Does not do it anymore	19%
25. Do you prefer rescue to fighting fire?	
a. yes	0%
b. no	88%
c. Likes both	12.5%
17. Of all the training you have had, what are you best at?	
a. Fighting fire	62.5%
b. Emergency rescue	12.5%
c. Both	12.5%
d. Fire inspection	6.2%
e. Administration	6.2%
19. Can anyone learn to be a fire fighter?	
a. yes	44%
b. no	56%

emergency rescue is less pronounced than their interest in fire fighting, and their self perception is that of a fire fighter who also happens to be an EMT or paramedic. They perceive themselves to be more dedicated to and better skilled at fire fighting than at emergency rescue.

The desire for advanced training is also a characteristic of a good fire fighter. Instructors and experienced fire fighters repeatedly admonish, "If you think you know it all, you're gonna get hurt." Because training is so much a part of their job and is considered an ongoing process, the fire fighters were asked if anyone could learn to be a fire fighter: 56% said "no" while 44% said "yes." Interestingly, both the positive and negative answers were qualified in the same way. In addition to good training, Johnny Butter said, very seriously, "It takes a special kind of person to be a fire fighter. Anyone can learn the mechanics of it, but not everyone can actually go and do it." The fire fighters think interest in doing a good job combined with training are essential to professional fire fighting. Training is linked to professionalism throughout the fire service, therefore any fire department with a large number of men certified in advanced training is perceived by the others to have great prestige. Through advanced training the Cows Crossing fire fighters want to be recognized for professionalism both in their own communities and in the wider community of fire fighters.

Characteristics of a good officer. Fire service officers are expected to be proficient in fire ground tactics, in administration and in handling personnel. Specific qualities include command ability, experience in fighting fire, ability to treat men equally and with respect and, finally, to be level headed (Table 9). A majority of respondents indicate many of these qualities are lacking in one or more of their own officers, particularly the chief. When the officers evaluated their own abilities, each captain expressed a desire for more leadership training.

Fire fighter code of ethics. In addition to the above characteristics, the fire fighters have developed a code of ethics or group norms by which they assess the worth of an individual fire fighter or assess the level of group solidarity. The norms are used to regulate daily interactions, to define unsatisfactory behavior, to reduce differences of opinion between men, and to deal with problems in role expectations.

Table 9 Qualities of a Good Officer	
Interview Question	Times Chosen (%)
16. What makes a good officer?	
a. Command ability, leadership, disciplinarian	75%
b. Experienced fire fighter	31%
c. Treat fire fighters equally	31%
d. Respect the fire fighters	25%
e. Level headed person/common sense	25%

This code combines with a more formal code of behavior taught to them at the fire college, and meshes with general community values, working class values and the male values discussed previously, to form the group norms (Table 10). The code is used to formulate group boundaries or social structure which the men earnestly maintain through their group rituals. These ethics or norms include: dedication and interest in fire fighting; willingness to learn the job and treat it as a career; teamwork; confidentiality and loyalty to the department; loyalty to other fire fighters; willingness to continue training; sharing the workload; confidence in one's ability; believing in the sanctity of womanhood; sexual prowess; abhorring homosexuality; being tough; respectability on and off duty; respecting other men's fire gear and personal vehicles; being able to take a joke and 'pay back'; and recognizing that rookies are not to give advice.

Training and Group Cohesion

As indicated above the fire fighters emphasize a need for ongoing training, which they equate with professionalism. Much of the training they are involved in explicitly or implicitly teaches them the importance of group cohesion or teamwork. Table 11 indicates the training classes open to fire fighters and the number of Cows Crossing men who have taken each class. The list is representative and not exhaustive. The Basic 200 Hours fire fighter class and the EMT (emergency medical technician) class are job requirements. During the research period several men were involved in the cardiopulmonary resuscitation class (CPR), the

Table 10
Values Which Contribute to the
Fire Fighters' Group Norms

Community Values

self-sufficiency
local autonomy
sense of history
neighborliness
public courtesy
sanctity of womanhood
priority of family/ church
caste/class system
respect for elders

Working Class Values

self-sufficiency
local autonomy
love of country
share work/pleasure along class lines
public courtesy
sanctity of womanhood
priority of kinship ties
class differentiation
division of labor along sex lines
job integrity
preference for male peer group
cult of sexual prowess for males
abhorrence of homosexuality
ability to "josh" within group

Male Values

cult of toughness
males suppress emotion
sanctity of womanhood
division labor along sex lines
importance of public (male) work over
    domestic (female)
preference for male peer group
cult of sexual prowess

Fire Fighter Group Norms

cult of toughness
    right to defend oneself,
      one's buddy, one's woman,
      one's property
    right to bear arms
    male suppression of emotion
job integrity
    dedication, willingness to work,
    believe in advanced training,
    departmental loyalty,
    'professionalism',
    respectability, self-confidence,
    teamwork
sanctity of womanhood
respect for elders
priority on family
caste/class differentiation
cult of sexual prowess
abhorrence of homosexuality
ability to take a joke, 'payback'
brotherhood of fire fighters

advanced cardiac life support class (ACLS), hazardous materials seminars, Hurst tool demonstrations (Jaws of Life), Smokedivers, paramedic training as well as the 200 Hours. One man is pursuing his degree in fire science. The classes with an asterisk are offered at institutions outside the community, while the others are taught either at the local hospital, community college or at the fire station. Seventy-two percent of the respondents indicate they want more training in fire combat or other fire related areas, while another 22% want more training in emergency rescue.

Table 11 Fire Fighting Training		
Class	No. Men Completing	No. Men Certified
Basic 200 Hours FF * **(b)**	18	18
Emergency Medical Technician (EMT) **(b)**	18	16
EMT Instructor	2	2
Cardiopulmonary Resus. (CPR)	18	16
CPR Instructor	9	8
First Aid	17	15
First Aid Instructor	5	4
Hazardous Materials	10	8
Hazardous Materials Instructor	1	1
Paramedic	5	4
Smokedivers*	4	4
Forest Fire*	5	2
Advanced Cardiac Life Support (ACLS)	9	9
Fire Science Degree*	1	—

Table: Indicates training only; the officers were trained as EMTs or paramedics, but did not run rescue.

(b) Mandatory for employment at the Cows Crossing Fire Department.

* Classes offered outside the community.

Some certifications, such as those earned by the completion of the 200 Hours or the EMT class are registered with a state regulatory agency. Other certifications are privately sponsored by fire safety companies or fire apparatus manufacturers including the hazardous materials training and the 35 hours practice with the Jaws of Life. Certification, with its attendant card, diploma or shirt patch, is important for accurate record keeping, the regulation by state fire standards, and are symbols of pride which the men display. Some certification requires periodic updating through refresher courses. These certifications include those for CPR (active for one year), EMT (active for four years), BLS (active for two years), ACLS (active for one year) and paramedic (active for one year). Specific fire fighting skills are kept active through local monthly drills and through participation in the Smoke-divers class at the state college.

The chief assigns the men to the training classes and attendance is mandatory. Attendance requires the rescheduling of duty hours, standby duty and cuts into the men's days off. Men cover for each other for the hours the classes meet; however, men in training are expected to return directly to duty at the conclusion of the class. Even the men who spend eight hours at the fire college return to the fire station to pull the remainder of their duty hours. During the entry level and advanced fire fighter training, the men are taught specific skills which enhance their teamwork on the job.

The State Fire College: Basic 200 Hours

Fire fighter training is designed to simulate the rigorous and unpredictable situations of actual fire and rescue incidents. Entry level and advanced fire fighters separately are taught new skills or are given the opportunity to hone previously learned skills. Under controlled situations individuals are pushed to their physical and mental limits to build self-confidence. However, the greatest imperatives stressed to all fire fighters are: (1) listen to your captain, (2) communicate with your partner (buddy), (3) learn to trust your equipment, and (4) learn to trust each other.

The 200 Hours class meets for eight hours a day, five days a week for five weeks. It begins at 7 a.m. with one hour of calisthenics, followed by classroom lecture. In the afternoon, the students practice with the equipment and participate in field evolutions (graduated drills).

The men are divided into four squads and competition between the squads is set up to force the men to rely on each other. The instructors are experienced fire fighters, some of whom conduct themselves like Marine drill instructors (DI); many are ex-military personnel. Men are praised for doing a good job, but they are derided for a poor performance. To deride them, the instructors call the trainees "pussies," "old women," or a "bunch of girls." The effect is to embarrass the men, while the goal is to make them strive harder on individual and team skills. Also individual derision brings squad pressure on the individual to try harder.

Throughout the drills, the trainees are repeatedly questioned by the instructors about what they are doing or where they are going. The instructors are concerned because "if a man isn't sure where he is, he could get lost in a building." Fire, smoke, noise from the water striking the walls, shouts and questions are all designed to simulate a fire scene in order to test the trainee's sense of direction, knowledge, self-confidence and trust in his buddy.

For the rookie fire fighters, the practical training in the smoke tower or in the burn building is essential, and frightening. They practice breathing with the mask and hose, and for those not used to breathing through a mask, it is difficult to place their faith in equipment which restricts breathing. Full air packs include the mask, hose and air tank, and are used only when smoke and fire are present. Adding to the confusion is a face mask which fogs up upon exhalation, heavy protective gear and cumbersome equipment (up to 65 pounds). The smoke and heat in the burn building is as intense as the shouts of the instructors who scream, "Keep your head down or your ears will melt! Keep that mask on! Talk to your buddy—where is your buddy? What's he doing? Keep your head down!"

The pressure to perform correctly as a team increases throughout the five weeks of training. By mid-term each squad identifies its weakest person and squads try to bring that man up to the level of the others. An instructor observed that the weakness of one fire fighter was covered up by the others: "He'll make it because the others are 'carrying' him."

Men are given the opportunity to master their skills and to achieve the level of proficiency necessary to pass the examination. However, no man is passed who does not meet state standards. For example, one man consistently lagged behind and required extra help from the instructors and encouragement from the other rookies. Finally, he acted in a manner which would have endangered the lives of fire fighters at an actual fire scene—he did not cooperate with his buddy in the building, but went off by himself. They decided he could not do a "man's job" and he was ostracized by the other trainees and dropped from the class.

The State Fire College: Smokedivers

Although none of the Cows Crossing fire fighters attended the Smokedivers class when I was there, 22% have attended in the past and more are scheduled. The Smokedivers class is eight hours a day for five days and, according to the instructors, is designed specifically to "push men to the limit, then take them beyond it." The men who participate are advanced fire fighters who have passed the 200 Hours or who have at least three years experience as fire fighters. The students I observed ranged in experience from eight months to twelve years.

Squads were chosen and competitive drills were instituted. The instructors use their usual DI voice, but these experienced fire fighters are not cowed by verbal abuse. One five year veteran said, "Once a man's been in a lot of fires and had the roof fall on his head, he is not frightened by these instructors." The men readily work in teams because they know from field experience that teamwork is the only way to get a job done with the least cost to life and property.

On the second day, they discussed what was the "key" to getting through the Smokedivers class. The men approached their training in the same manner they attacked a fire. They all wanted to complete the course, and since they were, as one student said, "brother firemen—not like the police who have to work alone"—they decided to "stick together." If one man were to "fall back," then the others would "carry him." These advanced fire fighters already learned the value of group cohesiveness so well that they could implement the notion of brotherhood quickly for highly specific reasons. This teamwork is what the entry level fire fighters worked weeks to achieve.

The physical strain on the last day is tremendous because it is an all day practical examination taken in full bunker gear. There were red faces, labored breathing and profuse sweating. The men made many trips to the stand pipe to wet their heads. Then the first man in the smoke tower test had a problem with his hose line. It knotted up. In his struggle to untangle the hose and finish the drill, he used up all his air. The bell on the air pack rang at mid-level on the stairs and he finished the last several minutes without air. He inhaled some smoke and when he got to the bottom of the tower he "fell out," which means he passed out and was sick. The other fire fighters revived him, made him rest for half an hour, then encouraged him to continue with the last portion of the test. With a paramedic following him, he successfully completed the examination. However, even if he had not completed the test, many of the other fire fighters stated he had earned his certification because he had done well consistently the previous days and he had not quit even after getting sick. He stands in contrast to the rookie fire fighter cited above.

The training available to fire fighters in the state exemplifies the attitude of the fire service in general and the CCFD fire fighter specifically: (1) a fire fighter must be given the best technical information and practical job skills available, (2) a fire fighter must be confident of his own ability, and (3) a fire fighter must learn to work as a team member.

The state fire training orientation manual contains guidelines for men who want to be accepted into a group where a family concept develops through eating, living and sharing time together while on duty. Men who want to be part of the brotherhood should express their dedication to and an interest in fire fighting and their loyalty to the fire service; they should believe in the importance of advanced training; maintain confidentiality regarding departmental affairs and they should be respectable on and off duty. The fire fighters are taught to believe that acceptance of these concepts will facilitate their acceptance into a group and will maintain a broad-based brotherhood of fire fighters.

Fighting Fire/Running Rescue in Cows Crossing

Fighting Fire

There are seasonal variations in activity, and late fall to late spring is the busiest time. Winter means an increase in the number of structure fires and other hazardous incidents. In 1978 the fire fighters responded to 107 alarms, including 43 structure fires (40%), 15 car fires (14%), 13 brush fires (12%) and 21 false alarms (19.6%). Fourteen percent of the fire calls were classified as "other" which included smoke scares and sprinkler systems malfunctions (Table 12). From January, 1979 to June 7, 1979, the fire fighters responded to 74 alarms, including 30 structure fires (40.5%), 14 brush fires (18.9%), 10 car fires (13.5%) and 16 false alarms (22%). There were also four hazardous materials incidents during that period such as gas station fires and railway chemical spills. In addition to these, the fire fighters responded to a bomb threat at the high school, and they "rolled" to all natural disaster sites, such as to the town marina which was partially destroyed by a tornado.

	Number/Percent of Total	
Table 12		
Fire Calls 1978–1979		
Type of Fire Call	1978 (12 mos)	1979 (6 mos)
Structure fires	43 (40%)	30 (40%)
Car fires	15 (14%)	10 (14%)
Brush fires	13 (12%)	14 (19%)
False alarms	21(20%)	16 (25%)
Other calls	15 (14%)	4
(smoke alarms, sprinkler system,		(less than 1%)
malfunctioning, etc.)		
Total Fire Calls	107	74
Total for Research Period: 181		

On Duty

The days almost always begin the same way. The men arrive between 7:30 and 8:00 in the morning to begin their 24 hour shift. The men going off duty usually gather in the kitchen with the arriving on-duty crew for coffee and a review of the previous day's events. At 8:00 the captain meets with the men to make job assignments.

At 9:00 station chores begin. Rescue units are checked by the men assigned to rescue that day. The equipment is tested, the supplies inventoried and the drug box checked. On the fire equipment, the engineer tests the lights, horn and siren and checks for the proper placement of tools and air packs. Small maintenance problems are handled at the station.

Housekeeping chores are begun in the morning as well. In addition to general cleanup, the men are assigned larger tasks by shift. "A" shift is responsible for the yard maintenance, "B" shift for waxing and polishing the floors, and "C" shift for cleaning the apparatus room where the engines and ambulances are kept.

Most of the station and housekeeping chores are completed by 10:30 unless a fire alarm or rescue call delays completion. After a man finishes his duties, he chooses another task or he "hides." Hiding means simply finding a corner somewhere behind the engines to sit down. This practice provides some private time for the men and it also keeps them out of the way of the captain who always has some task that needs doing

Some of the wives may come at noon to eat with the men, then from 1:00 to 5:00 the men finish their chores, study fire science, or emergency medical procedures, or "aggravate" each other. By afternoon they are supposed to change out of their work clothes and into their duty uniforms. The supper hour is from 5:00 to 7:00 After that the evening is "free time" during which the men study, read, talk, watch TV or play poker.

Inactive days, such as the one described above, when "we didn't even turn a wheel," are boring. The men dislike it and are often tense from the inactivity. Billy Bevis, a paramedic well respected by the others, said, "Being under constant tension all the time is physically tiring . . . sitting around waiting for something to happen just a phone call away and you never know what lies at the other end of it." Brad Whitehurst expressed the sentiments of several: "I'd rather have a good working fire every time I come to work. I enjoy fighting fire; I don't like sitting around "

According to the men, often long days of inactivity seem to result in long nights of rescue and fire operations. Johnny Butter occasionally is consulted about the possibility of a fire because his predictive abilities are amazingly accurate. If he predicts a fire for that night, some of the men go to bed early in preparation. Also, the fire fighters believe that the presence of a rookie on the shift means increased fire activity for several days. Such was the case in early March, 1979.

> **Case Study #1: Waiting for the Big One.** The men believe "fires come in bunches" and usually before daylight. For example, at 4:15 one morning, only one half hour after their return from a previous structure fire, another "working fire" broke out on the north side. The men were alerted by a coded "beep" simultaneously broadcast over the station intercom and the intercom systems located in each fire fighter's home. A voice said: "We have a signal 25 structure at the corner of 15th and B Street. All firemen report to the scene. Repeat, we have a signal 25 structure at the corner of 15th and B Street. All firemen report to the scene."

At the sound of the beeper tones, the men said a shot of adrenaline went through their systems. By the time the message was repeated, the on-duty fire fighters were bunkered up and mounted on Engines 5 and 7. Response time was less then two minutes. The off duty men and the volunteers used red flashers mounted on the dash of their cars to help get through any early morning traffic. Meanwhile, "Big Bertha" (the town siren) blared her hoarse, penetrating call. Ron Emmet, the rookie, explained, when "Big Bertha" is sounded, it means "we need all the help we can get."

Fires are never the same; the unexpected is always anticipated. Fire fighting procedures have to be flexible enough for adaptation to any situation. The men have no way of knowing in advance the layout of any home, nor if there are gas lines to the house, nor where the heating oil tanks are located, nor if there are people trapped inside the structure.

As the fire trucks rolled up to the scene, the fire fighters should have jumped off the tailboard of Engine 7 to "catch the hydrant" and hook the hose from the hydrant to the engine. However, the hydrant closest to the structure fire has no water. Therefore, Engine 5 also responded to the fire and was placed one block away from Engine 7. Through a series of reverse hose lays, the water was pumped from the functioning hydrant through Engine 5. This engine boosted the pressure to Engine 7, which then was supposed to "charge the attack lines" or fill the hoses with water. Nozzlemen stood ready to advance; they had to have water before they attacked because the house was "fully involved." A wide spray of water is used inside the structure not only to fight the fire but to protect the men from the heat and flames.

The engineer, Paul Jackson, was tense. He had pulled too close to the fire with Engine 7 and the intense heat had cracked the windshield. He had a dry hydrant and had to rely on a more complex system to get water to the fire fighters. Paul said later, "Without water to those men, very easily I could cook them inside of a fire in a few minutes. "

Still the men waited for water as the old frame house, made of heart pine (i.e., fatwood), burned more fiercely. The captain called for the deluge gun which is a specialized appliance attached to the top of Engine 7. The deluge gun can pump approximately 500 gallons per minute out of the engine. A fire fighter positioned himself to spray directly onto the roof of the structure. In one minute the fire fighter had drained the pumper and there was still no water to charge the hoses. The fire fighters all screamed for water. The engineer had forgotten to hook up the water supply from Engine 5. In another minute, however, the water supply was connected and the fire fighters began their attack.

The police had turned in the alarm and had cleared the area of traffic and onlookers shortly before the fire trucks arrived. After the hoses were laid, the police blocked off the streets to prevent onlookers from coming too close to the fire ground, and to prevent them from running over the hoses. The state Power and Light Company dispatched a lineman to cut the power to the house. Volunteer fire fighters worked with the paid men to extinguish the fire, or worked at the station in the dispatch office. One volunteer hooked up the auxiliary lights with a portable generator to illuminate the fireground for the fire fighters. There were a number of spectators, but everyone stayed out of the way. Many small groups of people looked concerned; they talked about the elderly, blind lady who lived in the house. Suddenly a woman screamed her grandmother's name and ran down the street to another house. By this time, the fire fighters and most of the onlookers realized the old woman had not gotten out of the house.

It seemed to take a long time to put the fire out, but in 25 minutes it was contained. The nozzles were shut down, but the hoses remained attached and charged until the house was dismantled. At 4:50 a.m. the fire was localized in the timbers and under the roof line. The men worked systematically through the house in search of the woman.

At 5:33 a.m. the fire fighters had not yet found the body, but several fire fighters and two policemen huddled in the front corner of the bedroom. They were quiet and from the looks on their faces and from the way some looked away, it was obvious they had found something. The woman had tried to escape, but had gone into her closet by mistake. All the fire fighters found were her charred remains. At 5:50 a.m. the funeral home arrived to bag the remains.

The fire fighters had "lost one" that night and they were unhappy. Afterwards, "J.W." Jones, a young captain said, "The hardest part about fire fighting is the rescue out of a burning building. You're in there, you've got your charged line or should have. You're trying to drag that around. You've got your full bunker gear and air pack on. There's this mental thing about you got to get 'em . . . there's somebody inside and you can't get to them . . . there's no way. You know they're already dead and there's nothing you can do." That is what diminishes the joy and satisfaction of fire fighting for these men.

Reportedly adrenaline levels dropped toward the end of the fire combat. Salvage and overhaul were difficult, dirty, and time consuming. Salvageable property was turned over to the survivors and every corner of the structure was examined for pockets of fire.

At 6:40 a.m., back at the station, teams of men washed the canvas hoses and coiled them on the drying rack for placement in the drying oven. Others reloaded the hose beds of Engines 5 and 7 with dry hoses. The engines were wiped down, refilled with water and repositioned in the bay of the station in readiness for the next alarm. One man refilled the air packs, while others cleaned their face masks or hosed off their bunder gear. Most of the men were dirty and it would take several days to cough up the smoke some of them had "eaten."

The fire fighters were wet and cold, tired and hungry. Some volunteers left for their regular jobs, some fire fighters prepared to "pull duty" that day, and most of these men had already responded to the small structure fire at a downtown hotel earlier that morning.

There was very little horseplay after this fire. Some men displayed their burned helmets and talked about the fire. In an effort to cheer up, the rookie was singled out as the cause of the two fires that night. His head was flushed in the toilet, but the men showed little enthusiasm for their ritual. It was a long time before the term "crispy critter," referring to a burned person, was used again at the fire station.

Other fires—"the only ones worth discussing"—are the working fires in which life and property are saved. These are more "fun" to fight because they are a positive challenge. The work is difficult, the smoke thick and dangerous and the salvage and overhaul wet and tiring: however, a successfully fought fire is an occasion for happiness. Breakfast tastes better, the chief is happy and the fire fighters joke and horse around. It is an occasion to talk about a job well done. According to Billy Joe Cellon, the oldest captain,

> That is the best part of fire fighting—seeing a job well done. A fire stopped in its early stages—quick attack, quick knockdown. You get a feeling of accomplishment because you've done something. Perhaps saved somebody's life, somebody's property that they worked for all their life to get.

Deakin sums up the feelings of the fire fighters: " . . . the unpredictability and urgency of the emergencies made the rest of their work relatively boring . . . But they were ready to sacrifice the possibility of finding alternative meaningful work and organized activity for the excitement and involvement of fire fighting itself" (1977:466).

The fire fighters are called upon to respond to increasingly complex fire emergencies. Hazardous materials incidents are increasing in the county and the fire department is concerned because the men must respond to incidents involving extremely toxic chemicals. Chemicals are used in many of the manufacturing plants in the city and the railroad routinely freights hazardous materials through the center of town. During the observation period the men dealt with an ammonia leak in a meat packing plant, a chemical spill which resulted from a train wreck and faced the possibility of being burned by acid from a home made burglar system placed above the door frame. Often the men respond to these incidents without proper protective gear, equipment or training.

Structure fires, explosions, hazardous materials incidents, and even brush fires, involve the unknown—a challenge which must be met with calm, skill and courage. The men enjoy "clean fire fighting" where no human lives are lost. They prefer fire fighting over emergency rescue, however, there are more emergency runs in one week than there are fires to fight, and the emergency services provide a different challenge.

Running Rescue

Emergency rescue takes up the larger portion of the men's time. Rescues are handled by the on-duty crew, while transfers to hospitals out of the county are handled by a standby crew of two men. In thirteen and one half months, the fire fighters responded to 2,060 emergency calls. In addition, they responded to 576 more calls which are classified as 10–22 (disregard) or 10–66 (cancelled). The average number of calls per week, not including these, is about 40. Of the total number of actual emergency calls (2060), 53% were "sickness" and .08% were "injury" (Table 13). There were 24% "transfers" between hospitals and homes, to hospitals outside the county or to other health facilities both within and outside the county. Also common were "Signal 4" calls (traffic accidents, 10%), "Signal 7" (death, 0.2%), "pregnant women" (.01%) and "crazy people" (.005%). There were isolated incidents such as drownings, boat accidents, injuries at public events, disasters resulting from storms, and the birth of babies. As Brad Whitehurst said, "There is no doubt that rescue breaks up the monotony."

Some calls that break up the monotony are unappreciated by the fire fighters and are a major source of frustration for them. These are the "lizard runs." Brad expressed the annoyance of most of the fire fighters by saying, "I don't mind a worthwhile call, but I hate to get woke up in the night to go look at somebody's hurt toe. That's not an emergency and they don't need an ambulance. That's a lizard run." Pete, Brad's riding partner, elaborated by saying the fire fighters resent their being used as a "taxi service by people who don't really need a rescue, by those who have two cars sitting in the yard."

Fire fighters in the role of certified emergency medical technicians or paramedics are expected to make split second decisions affecting the lives of their patients. They are held accountable for their rescue efforts and are expected to react within the confines of their training and certification. "Heroic"

Table 13 Rescue Calls 1978–1979*		
Type of Rescue Call	Number/Percent of Total	
Sickness	1097	(53%)
Transfers	485	(24%)
Signal 4	216	(10%)
Injury	168	(.08%)
10-7 (death)	45	(.02%)
Pregnant woman	37	(.01%)
"Crazy" people	12	(.005%)
Total Actual Emergencies: 2060		
10-22 / 10-66 (disregard call)	576	(22%)
Total Rescue Calls: 2636		
*13.5 months time		

measures in the field are considered medically unsound and are officially discouraged by the fire department and the emergency medical system because they may exceed the training of the EMT or paramedic.

In Cows Crossing, however, a local physician assumes responsibility for the EMTs and paramedics and his malpractice insurance covers them while they are on duty. He works full time in the emergency room of the hospital and helps with the men's classroom and practical training. With his whole-hearted support for the EMS system and his daily involvement in it, reportedly the men sometimes exceed their official certification to save lives. For example, certain EMTs who are trusted by the physician start IVs, intubate patients or administer drugs with the knowledge and approval of the physician. Clearly, there is variation in individual capabilities which the physician recognizes and utilizes. However, such procedures may leave the men open to lawsuits, despite the physician's observance or coverage

Case Study #2: Signal 4. As with fires, there is nothing typical about a rescue. Some of the most spectacular and challenging are the "Signal 4" traffic accidents, which may entail any sort of injury. For example, at

10:30 p.m. in late May, 1979, the fire fighters were called to an accident on the road between Cows Crossing and Potato City. A car with two people in it had been broadsided by a bus carrying eleven migrant laborers. Initially, one rescue unit was dispatched carrying two experienced EMTs and one EMT trainee.

When the rescue unit arrived, two passersby were administering CPR to the driver of the car. His passenger was lying injured in a ditch of waist high water. Among the migrant laborers there appeared to be fractures and lacerations. The EMT-driver radioed for more units. Triage procedures were instituted by the EMTs during which they judged who was the most seriously hurt; those bleeding or having breathing difficulties were treated first.

The man being given CPR was so severely injured that he bled with every breath being pumped into him. There was no heart function so one EMT instructed the men to discontinue CPR. The man was dead. This EMT and the trainee turned to the injured woman in the ditch. After examination they determined a possible broken neck, slipped a neck brace and a back board on her and removed her from the ditch. Her broken leg was splinted, then she was loaded into the ambulance.

By the time the woman had been attended to the EMT-driver had administered aid to the migrant laborers. Additional medical assistance (i.e., mutual aid) had been rendered from a rescue unit in Potato City, from three more units from Cows Crossing, from one unit located in a city 30 miles away and from a unit located in a city 75 miles away. This latter unit was manned by a former Cows Crossing fire fighter who was on a return run from a transfer of his own, and who responded to the call on his radio.

En route to the hospital in Cows Crossing, the EMTs radioed the condition of their patients so the emergency room would be prepared. At the hospital, responsibility for the patients was turned over to the emergency room staff.

Sometimes rescue personnel are called to the scene of family quarrels or to barroom brawls. The men are supposed to have police protection in these cases, but occasionally they arrive ahead of the police. Stress is created by their not knowing the exact nature of the situation, nor if onlookers will prevent them from treating the patient, nor if they also will be attacked.

Case Study #3: Family Violence. Rescue workers were called to the scene of a family quarrel in which a woman had been shot. The police were alerted also but did not arrive before the ambulance. The EMTs initiated rescue procedures, and then heard a shotgun being pumped in the next room. A man said, "I didn't shoot the motherfuckin' bitch for you to fix up." The EMTs left the house immediately to wait for the police. By the time all the officials were able to re-enter the house, the woman was dead.

The Cows Crossing Fire Department is a very busy rural station which tries to meet the fire and emergency rescue needs of a fairly large geographical area, as well as participate officially in community events (Table 14). The department is organized along paramilitary lines and contains many of the ranks found in military units. The chief is the commander of the department, but his paternalistic interpretation of his role conflicts with the expectations the fire fighters have for strong leadership. The assistant chief is caught between the chief's arbitrariness and the fire fighters' mounting frustration with what they perceive to be a lack of discipline and professionalism at the station. These organizational conflicts, plus the nature of the job of fighting fire, create stress among the men. These topics are discussed in the following chapter.

Table 14
Calendar of Events

List includes official functions and training events. Does not include shift dinners on major holidays or family events.

* June 1978
Sailing Regatta

July 1978
July 4th Parade
200 Hours Class (5 weeks)

August 1978
Training Drill
200 hours Class cont.

September 1978
Paramedic Class (27 weeks)
200 Hours Class (5 weeks)
Smokedivers (1 week)
EMT Cass (5 weeks)
Homecoming Parade

October 1978
Paramedic Class cont.
200 Hours Class cont.
200 Hours Class (5 weeks)
EMT Cass cont.

November 1978
Paramedic Class cont.
200 Hours Class cont.
Smokedivers (1 week)

December 1978
Paramedic Class cont.
Smokedivers (1 week)
Christmas parade

* June 1978 beginning of observation
  and data gathering

January 1979
Paramedic Class cont.
EMT Class (5 weeks)
Station Dinner

February 1979
Paramedic Class cont.
200 Hours Class (5 weeks)
Smokedivers (1 week)
EMT Class cont.
Hazardous Materials Seminar
Country Fair Booth (1 week)

March 1979
Paramedic Class cont.
200 Hours Class cont.
Smokedivers (1 week)
Flower Festival Parade
Boat Races on the River
'Jaws of Life' Training

April 1979
Paramedic Class cont.
200 Basic Class (5 weeks)
EMT Class (5 weeks)
Rodeo Parade Rodeo

May 1979
Paramedic Class cont.
200 Hours Class cont.
Smokedivers (1 week)
EMT Class cont.
Mother's Day Dinner
Senior Citizens' Parade

June 1979
Paramedic Class cont.

7

STRESS: RITUAL AND NON-RITUAL COPING PROCESSES

Individual Stress

The discussion on stress is largely based on Selye's initial description of individual stress, which he divides into two parts: eustress and distress (Selye, 1970). Eustress is a positive force which motivates humans to work, create and live while distress is harmful and is considered disease-producing if sustained over long periods of time. For example, the diseases suffered by fire fighters such as heart attacks, lower back problems, high blood pressure may be the result of prolonged stress. The general adaptation syndrome (G.A.S.) which develops in response to stress has three stages: alarm, resistance to the stress and exhaustion if the stress is not alleviated.

Kahn (1969:34) explored the relationship of men's jobs and their health to the stress of organization life. Role conflicts, shift work, job status, self-esteem and other self identified stressors are factors related to job stress and interpersonal relationships. Individuals who are stressed by organizational dysfunction, poor leadership and alternate periods of hazardous duty and boredom may use ritual processes to relieve the tensions and to promote social solidarity (Spradley, personal communication).

It is important to examine stress among the fire fighters because they are expected to react to disaster as a team, calmly and knowledgeably. As individuals they work long hours under hazardous conditions, they must exert a great deal of energy and they must endure the horrors of their job. Without a release from their stress, I believe they would not be able to work together effectively.

Stress Seekers/Crisis Stress/Social Responsibility

Using the basic research on stress, Tanner (1976) describes stress seekers, crisis stress and the role of social responsibility during times of stress. Stress seekers are persons who deliberately seek stress because it brings a feeling of being alive (see Selye's "deprivation stress," 1978:385–386). Further, stress seekers choose an adversary which can be challenged successfully. Crisis stress is an event in which there is danger plus an opportunity to meet a challenge. However, the drastic change involved in crisis stress may be harmful if met alone, or it may be beneficial if an individual meets it as part of a group effort. The group effort basic to fire fighting likely is beneficial to individuals because it contributes to a feeling of heightened group solidarity. Feelings of social responsibility are important characteristics of the Cows Crossing fire fighters. These men meet the challenge of a wide variety of emergencies and their failure to measure up to their responsibility weighs heavily on certain individuals and on the group. Both personal pride and group esteem or group image are important factors in social responsibility. Responsibility and a sense of personal pride are part of the job satisfaction the fire fighters express and are thought to be achieved through individual competence and group solidarity.

Stress, Crisis and Behavior

One stress model comprising stress, crisis and behavior is useful because it goes beyond biological responses to stress and into individual social responses to stress (du Toit, 1979). The author "suggests that certain events may precipitate periods of stress, that these are apt to build up due to heightened anxiety (or may decrease due to a process of coping) and that this leads to stressful behavior" (du Toit, 1979:119). He concludes that stress can be frequent, cyclic or chronic, but it cannot be borne indefinitely. After a discussion of the hazards and of the stress involved in fire fighting at Cows Crossing, I adapt du Toit's model in the present research in two places: to diagram individual response to anticipatory stress and the excitement of fire fighting; and to describe group mechanisms for solving a problem.

When analyzing the stress evident in the study group, the interrelationship between individual stress, family problems, and intra-organizational problems must be kept in mind. It is easy to isolate instances of stress for discussion, but one type of stress does feed into another, or, more precisely, one stressed person may create stress responses by members of his family or by members of the group with which he works. This domino effect of stress responses may damage the cohesiveness of the working unit.

Hazards of The Job

The specific items which the fire fighters find stressful are categorized as individual problems. They include physical and emotional stress, family problems and organizational problems. Fire fighting in America is considered the most hazardous occupation as demonstrated by the 1978 National Fire Prevention Association (NFPA) statistics on injuries. The NFPA estimates there were 106,897 fire fighter injuries in the U.S. in 1978, and 162 fire fighter deaths (Karter, 1979:14). In the South, the annual average number of injuries per fire department was reported as 4.9, while the average number of injuries per 100 structure fires was 5.3 (Karter, 1979:16). These averages for the South are less than the national average, and the average for Cows Crossing was less than the average for the South. For 1978, of the 66,907 injuries reported nationally, 32.3% were caused from exposure to fire products, 1.5% to structural collapse, 4.8% to exposure to radiation or hazardous materials, 35.4% to falls or to being struck by an object, and 11.5% to "stress" including overexertion. Fourteen and one-half percent of the injuries were due to "other" causes, not specified (Karter, 1979:14–15). Table 15 is a typology of fire fighting hazards; this is a representative table and not exhaustive. Hazards are complicated by the type and condition of fire fighting equipment and by weather conditions.

Fire fighter injuries during 1978 were high for the nation, although in Cows Crossing only two men performed restricted duty because of injuries; one had a broken arm, the other a broken foot. When men suffer cuts, bruises and burns, work assignments are not altered for them. Even fire fighters with broken limbs are expected to report for duty and spend their time in the watchroom operating the dispatch.

The activities involved in fighting a fire are perceived as the most hazardous part of the dual job at Cows Crossing and are tabulated on Table 16. Fighting fire, hazardous materials incidents and the "unknown" at a fire are cited most often as the greatest hazards the fire fighters face. Tommy Lee, a young fire fighter, said,

> The hazards? It's got to be the fire fighting end of it. Going into a burning building that's got a lot of smoke in it, a lot of fumes and gases. If you don't have a good seal on your air pack, you're leaving yourself wide open to get killed or hurt.

Table 15
Typology of Fire Fighting/Emergency Rescue Hazards

Fire Fighting Hazards *
Initial attack and knockdown of fire
Driving the fire trucks, engines
Fire rescue out of a burning building
Hazardous materials incidents
Equipment failure
Structural collapse
Injury by falling or object hitting fire fighter
Exposure to fire products
Heat exhaustion, physical stress/strain

Emergency Rescue Hazards
Driving the ambulance
Hostile bystanders
        family violence
        public fights
Combative patients
        drug overdosed
        drunks
        "crazy" people
Emotional stress/strain

* This list is representative and not exhaustive; other hazards
are combinations of the above categories. Hazards are also
complicated by the type and condition of equipment used
and by weather conditions.

An officer, Billy Joe Cellon, reports, "Things you can't anticipate, which is part of the job. Every fire has its own personality.
You cannot walk up to a building and see a fire and say, 'I know
what it's all about on this fire.'" This anticipation of the unknown is particularly important because of the increased inci-
dences of hazardous materials spills and fires. The unknown in a
fire situation is complicated severely by the unstable conditions

```
┌─────────────────────────────────────────────────────────────┐
│                         Table 16                             │
│                  Hazards of Fire Fighting                    │
│                                                             │
│  Interview Questions                       Times Chosen (%)  │
│                                                             │
│  7.  What is the most hazardous part of your job?           │
│       a.  Fire fighting                         37.5%        │
│       b.  10–18 ambulance runs                  37.5%        │
│       c.  Hazardous materials incidents         12.5%        │
│       d.  "Unknown" at a fire                    6.0%        │
│       e.  Fire rescue                            6.0%        │
│                                                             │
│  8.  Do you have the equipment necessary to meet the hazards │
│       of your job?                                          │
│       a.  yes                                   12.5%        │
│       b.  no                                    50.0%        │
│       c.  Qualified yes                         37.5%        │
│                                                             │
└─────────────────────────────────────────────────────────────┘
```

of many chemicals and the use of synthetic materials in furniture, carpets and draperies. Another hazard cited by 37.5% of the men is running ambulance calls, particularly the "10-18 runs" which means "with all due speed." Paul Jackson, an engineer who is responsible for getting the fire apparatus to the fire scene, says this:

> It would have to be the highway . . . getting to the scene of the fire or accident. People have air conditioned cars, they keep their radio turned up and fail to hear the siren. It causes more problems than what the fire or other emergency actually causes us. People fail to give the right of way to us, don't hear the sirens, make a left turn in front of us, run through red lights. Running to the scene can really pucker you.

Questioning the men about the hazards of their work led into a question about whether the equipment available for their use is adequate to help them do their job. Generally, at the Cows Crossing Fire Department, the equipment is old and worn and 50% of the men stated they do not have the equipment necessary to meet the hazards of their job. An additional 37.5% qualified their negative answers by stating that specific pieces of equipment need to be replaced or updated. Of the many complaints, two are outstanding because of their direct bearing on the personal safety of each fire fighter: the breathing apparatus and the protective gear. Sam Turner was particularly critical, "Four or five breathing apparatus out there are outlawed by federal law, but we cannot take them out of service because we are so short. They are ineffective." The men who criticize the quality of their equipment believe that if the community, or specifically the commissioners, had more respect for the fire department their equipment would be updated. Having good equipment has historically been a point of pride for fire fighters, but is also a point of safety for the Cows Crossing men.

Many pieces of protective gear have holes in them or they fit improperly. Further, none of the gear is designed to protect the men against hazardous materials incidents, although through a system of mutual aid, men with proper protective gear could be obtained from outside the county within an hour. The men maintain, however, that they should be provided with the proper gear in order to protect themselves while they are trying to protect the community.

Physical Stress

Fire fighters voluntarily expose themselves to life threat in the disciplined performance of duty, and in so doing, episodic demands (i.e., stressful), are made on them. The physical and emotional stress they face is intensive, but is not a constant 24-hour a day pressure. Periods of intense activity are balanced by periods of boredom, a state which brings its own form of stress.

Physical exertion is cited by 75% of the men as greatest in fighting fire and 12.5% specified fire rescue as the most physically stressful (Table 17). Some men report that actual combat is exhausting because of a combination of intense heat, smoke, restricted breathing and the weight of the protective gear. Others say the salvage and overhaul at the scene, and reloading the engines at the station are worse because adrenaline levels are lowest then. What is required of each man is that he be capable of short bursts of physical exertion in fighting the fire or rescuing a victim, followed by sustained heavy labor during salvage and overhaul and reloading the equipment. The threat of heat exhaustion from the fire and from the southern climate compounds the stress.

Table 17
Physical/Emotional Stressors in Fire Fighting

Interview Questions	Times Chosen (%)
11. What is the most physically stressful part of your job?	
a. Fighting a fire	75.0%
b. Rescue at a fire	12.5%
c. Car wrecks	12.5%
13. What is the most emotionally stressful part of your job?	
a. Death/injury of a child	50.0%
b. Rescue of a known person	18.7%
c. Personnel conflicts at station	18.7%
d. Lizard runs	6.0%

Emotional Stress

Anticipation of an event is central to the job of fire fighting and as a first response unit to all disasters, the fire fighters have to maintain readiness for their entire 24 hour shift. Anticipation amplifies stress because both the brain and the body must be alert. For some of the fire fighters the anticipation of an event is more stressful than the event itself, and they refer to these anticipatory states as "boredom."

Fifty percent of the men cite the death or injury of a child as the greatest emotional stress, particularly so for the men who have children (Table 17). Paul Jackson, an engineer, recalls:

The loss of somebody that you know. They died in your hands while you were working with them. I would say that tends to tear you up. Or seeing small children like the wreck we went to a couple of years back. We were taking the parents out of the car along with two children. We know the people and we knew they only had two children, so we got them out and they was comfortable. The husband said, "My baby!" We called the names of the two children and he said, "No, my new baby!" We didn't know that he was coming back from the city from adopting a new baby. And we started looking through the car and we found the baby underneath the front seat of the car. The baby was dead. That does get next to you.

Other stressful situations occur for 18.7% of the men when they have to rescue persons known to them. This happens frequently in a small town and the men feel it is difficult for them to remain dispassionate and impersonal in their rescue attempts.

Intragroup problems are also stressful for 18.7% of the fire fighters. Other stressors are those found in dealing with combative patients such as those who are drug overdosed, fight victims, or mentally ill. Delivering babies in the ambulance while en route to the hospital, completing a rescue in the presence of hostile onlookers and dealing with hysterical parents whose children have been injured are also stressful to the fire fighters.

Individual Coping Processes

Clearly the externally imposed stress placed on these individuals is episodic and intense. They use a variety of mechanisms for relieving the stress (Table 18). In greater than 60% of the cases the men reportedly deal with this personal stress by suppressing it. Billy Joe Cellon, the oldest captain, said, "You have to suppress it. If you don't, it will get you down. You can't function the way you should. You suppress it."

It is reported to be unusual for a fire fighter to be sent home because of the emotional effects of a bad rescue call. For example, only two men in the past ten years reportedly have been excused from duty after one unsuccessful attempt to rescue two children trapped in a burning car. Most fire fighters say that they discuss the death and injury of children, as well as other selected topics, with their wives. Two men indicate that a physical workout is their therapy.

Although only one man reports joking as a means of tension release, a majority of the men have been observed joking with each other on many occasions about "Signal 4s" (traffic accidents), "crispy critters" (burned people), and about "lizard runs" (non-emergency ambulance calls). With regard to the bad rescue or fire calls in which someone is hurt or killed, Pete Johnson reasoned, "If you can't kid about it, you'll go crazy."

On a psychological level, Hegge and Marlow (1979) have found that fire fighters have developed individual mechanisms for mitigating stress, such as selective inattention to certain classes of environmental stimuli which would normally elicit stress.

Table 18
Coping With Stress

Interview Questions	Times Chosen (%)
14. How do you deal with your stress?	
a. Suppress the emotion	56.0%
b. Talk it over with my wife	12.5%
c. Physical workout	12.5%
d. Rest	6.0%
e. Joking	6.0%
f. Nothing	6.0%
15. What do you discuss with other fire fighters?	
a. Methods, procedures in fire fighting	68.7%
b. Administrative problems	31.3%

The fire fighters in Cows Crossing refer to this as "not thinking about the danger," or "not dwelling on the risks." The men's suppression of feelings is consistent with their feelings about their personal safety on the job. Eighty-seven percent of the men report they either do not worry about their own safety or worry only "sometimes" or "seldom" (Table 19). These men feel there is no need to worry as long as they understand their job and exercise caution. Brad Whitehurst, a hazardous materials instructor, maintains there is no need for worry as long as "you don't get in so far that you can't get out [of a structure fire], and you go back to the basics [of fire fighting] to save yourself." The men report they are too busy to think about the risks they face until the conversation after the fire back in the watchroom. They apparently differentiate between the stress of fire fighting and worry about their safety; in their minds the two are not related.

Worry is alleviated also because no fire fighter is required to place himself in a situation in which he believes he could lose his own life and no officer should knowingly order his men into extremely dangerous situations. Their attitude is that property is less valuable than human life.

Table 19
Fire Fighters' Concerns About Safety

Interview Questions	Times Chosen (%)
21. Do you worry about your safety on the .job?	
a. yes	12.5%
b. no	50.0%
c. sometimes, seldom	37.5%

Only Johnny Butter is considered by the others to be a risk-taker. He has gone into structure fires alone and fallen through the floor, and he went onto a weakened roof at another fire and fell through it. He had to be rescued by the others in both cases. The other fire fighters respect his fearlessness, but work with him cautiously so as not to endanger themselves.

Anticipatory stress, or what the fire fighters refer to as "boredom," is relieved by the challenge of crisis stress. Here du Toit's (1979) model is proposed for discussing crisis, stress and behavior and is adapted schematically to a situation involving a hypothetical fire fighter (Diagram 1). In general the stress fire fighters face may be measured on a continuum with anticipation at one end, peaks of situational stress along it and exhaustion at the other end. The stressor is the anticipation of a disaster which results in a continuous state of mental and physical readiness. Actual fire combat is one peak of stress, which is challenged by the mediating factors of adrenaline levels, training and group effort.

The alarm or call to action is the precipitating event. Officers and fire fighters initially appraise the crisis situation as the engine nears the fire. General anxiety is reduced if the fire fighter arrives too late to save the structure of if there is a false alarm. Adrenaline level is high, and he remains keyed up, but this keying up is controlled.

The fire fighter may perceive a threat to his life as he approaches or enters the fire and this may increase his anxiety level. If it does, a secondary appraisal of the situation occurs as the fire fighter attempts to match his training to the challenge.

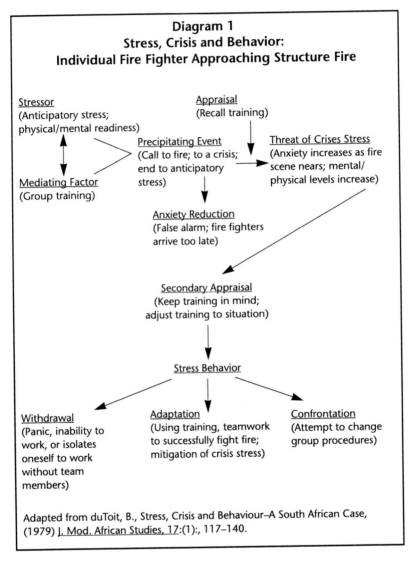

Diagram 1
Stress, Crisis and Behavior:
Individual Fire Fighter Approaching Structure Fire

Stressor
(Anticipatory stress;
physical/mental readiness)

Appraisal
(Recall training)

Precipitating Event
(Call to fire; to a crisis;
end to anticipatory
stress)

Threat of Crises Stress
(Anxiety increases as fire
scene nears; mental/
physical levels increase)

Mediating Factor
(Group training)

Anxiety Reduction
(False alarm; fire fighters
arrive too late)

Secondary Appraisal
(Keep training in mind;
adjust training to situation)

Stress Behavior

Withdrawal
(Panic, inability to
work, or isolates
oneself to work
without team
members)

Adaptation
(Using training, teamwork
to successfully fight fire;
mitigation of crisis stress)

Confrontation
(Attempt to change
group procedures)

Adapted from duToit, B., Stress, Crisis and Behaviour–A South African Case,
(1979) J. Mod. African Studies, 17:(1):, 117–140.

At the fire scene, the fire fighter may choose one of three stress behaviors as depicted by du Toit. A successful adaptation to the stress would manifest itself through the fire fighter's effective completion of his task. Alternatively, he may panic and withdraw from the challenge of fighting the fire. Withdrawal may be defined also as a fire fighter's isolating himself from the team to fight the fire alone. A third choice at the fire scene is confrontation which might be interpreted by the others as "not following orders" or insubordination. Both withdrawal and confrontation may be interpreted by other fire fighters as forms of panic or uncontrolled behavior and thus as being overcome by the stress of the situation. A fire fighter may more successfully challenge group fire fighting procedures during the discussion after the fire. Such a successful confrontation may serve to relieve some of the anxiety he feels at the next fire.

It is proposed that a fire fighter might successfully engage in two or more of the stress behaviors discussed above. Fire, particularly structure fires, can be complicated and unpredictable, requiring individual fire fighters to be alert and flexible in their stress behavior as they enter, exit and re-enter a structure fire.

Family Problems and Fire Fighter Stress

Fire fighter couples face stressors which are extensions of the hazards involved in fire fighting. The wives worry about their husbands and the fire fighters worry about their families when they are on duty. Couples have devised individual methods for coping with stress, and the fire department provides formal and informal situations in which this stress is mitigated.

The fifteen women who participated in the study answered 51 questions about fire fighting and their relationship to it (Appendix B). These women range in age from 19–35 years, with the average at 25 years. Ninety-three percent are married and of those, 20% are divorced and remarried. One woman is single (divorced), but has a long standing relationship with "her fire fighter."

The women who married fire fighters are often reminded by the fire fighters that they not only married a man, but married an entire department or an occupation. Their families are important to the men, but fire fighting has a greater priority in many cases. Family life is scheduled around the fire fighter's occupation. The demands of the job—long hours and strenuous work—often means family relations take a second place. Many of the women were introduced to fire fighting as young girls, and are aware of the problems such an occupation could pose on family life. Fifty-three percent of the women indicate they have either a father, uncle, grandfather, cousin or female relative who has been a fire fighter.

The men's low pay means that 67% of the women have jobs outside the home; the need to have their wives work to make ends meet is very real, and, in general, the men support the idea of both adults working. This attitude stands in contrast to the generally accepted working class notion that women should remain in the home (LeMasters, 1975:45). Of those women who work outside the home, 40% work 30 hours or fewer, while 60% work 40 hours or more each week.

Scheduling time together is difficult for the fire fighter couples. Of the ten women who work, 40% have flexible hours so it is possible for them to coincide their work schedules with their husband's. Sixty percent had fixed hours and had to "adjust" or "do the best we can" in coordinating leisure time together. It is not surprising that 46% of the women report they do not have enough time with their fire fighters, while an additional 13% say they "sometimes" have enough time together. Long hours apart and long hours together are normal for fire fighter couples. However, such work schedules are stressful, particularly for purposes of socializing.

Coping With Family Problems

Job stress and the mitigation of that stress is a major factor in the relationships between the women and their fire fighters. The women are aware that their husbands are involved in the most hazardous occupation in the U.S. and have to mitigate their own worry over that situation. In addition, the women believe they have to deal with the men's fatigue, their frustration with the administration or with personal relations among the men, and with any emotional stress from bad rescue calls.

The effect of individual stress on the family and on the relationships between each man and his mate is explored through the women's answers to questions on the following topics: (1) their perception of their husband's likes and dislikes about the job, (2) their worries about the nature of their husband's occupation, (3) their discussions with their husbands about the job of fire fighting, (4) their discussions with other wives about the job of fire fighting, and (5) their own personal interest in fire fighting and emergency medical training. The underlying assumption for these questions is that the more the wives are able to understand and identify with their husband's job, the less stress the couples will have to mitigate (Fjelstad, 1978:77). It should be noted at the outset, however, that this is a group of relatively young couples and for most of them it is their first experience in dealing with a job of this nature. What the data below indicate is that these couples are involved in the process of becoming adjusted to the job, and that their identification with it may come with time and experience.

First, the women state most often that their fire fighters like "saving lives," "helping people," and "fighting fire." More specifically, 87% of the women liked the idea of their husband's being a fire fighter. Sixty-seven percent of the positive responses are explained like this: "His job gives him satisfaction and a sense of accomplishment, making him happy, therefore making me happy." Twenty-seven percent of the respondents cite humanitarian reasons for liking their husband's work as did one wife who said, "It's important that people want to help people. It makes me proud to tell others the work he does."

The least liked aspects of their job are categorized as the administrative problems (60%) such as the standby system, low pay, and personal relations with the other men. Specifically, "rescue" or ambulance runs are cited by 27% of the women as the single aspect the least liked by the men (Table 20).

Second, in spite of the apparent support the women indicate for their husband's occupation, 80% worry about their men while they are on duty (Table 20). Frequently, those wives who worry the most eventually become non-supportive of their husband's job and the men resign from the station. Fjelstad (1978:76) also noted a high level of stress among fire fighter's wives directly related to the hazards of their husband's occupation.

The Cows Crossing women were asked to specify what they worried about, but expressed themselves only in general terms. They worried about the "unknown" or about their fire fighter's "getting hurt." However, one woman said, "that he may never come home. Anything can happen at a fire or a rescue call."

When the women worry about their fire fighters, 40% wait for some word about the men from the station or they monitor the situation on the scanner (Table 21). The scanner is commonly used by both fire fighters and their wives to keep in touch with events at the station or around the county. Eighty-seven percent have one in their homes and keep it on constantly when the men are on duty or on standby. Some women complain about the intrusiveness of the "black monster," but are resigned to its presence. Additionally, when the men are at a fire scene or an accident, some of the wives go to the station or phone. This latter

Table 20
Wives' Attitudes About Husband's Vocation

Interview Questions	Times Chosen (%)
47. What does your fire fighter like best about what he does?	
a. Saving lives, helping people	60.0%
b. Fighting fires	33.3%
c. Fire prevention/education	6.6%
48. What does your fire fighter like least about what he does?	
a. Administrative problems	60.0%
b. Rescue, ambulance runs	27.0%
c. Death	13.0%
41. Do you like the fact that your man is a fire fighter?	
a. yes	87.0%
b. no	13.0%
42. Do you like the work he does?	
a. yes	87.0%
b. no	13.0%

is common after a fire, when perhaps half the wives wait in the parking lot or in the reception room at the station until the men complete the cleanup.

Sixty-three percent of the fire fighters worry about their wives and families while they are on duty (Table 22). They worry about their general safety at home or while traveling in a car. Fifty-three percent of the men who worry allay their fears by phoning their wives, while 10% report "suppressing" any worry they have about their families. None of the women expressed any worry about their being alone at night. However, my observations indicate that for at least three of the women it is a problem. Two often stay at their mother's house on duty night.

Third, the wives are kept abreast of events at the fire station through their husbands, which helps them understand what their husbands face daily. Thirty-one and one-third percent of the fire fighters state they discuss "everything" with their wives,

---

Table 21
Wives Concerns About Husbands Safety

Interview Questions	Times Chosen (%)
44. Do you worry about your fire fighter when he is on a rescue run or at a fire? **(a)**	
a. yes	80%
b. no	20%
36. Do you listen to a scanner when he is on duty? **(a)**	
a. yes	87%
b. no	13%

Table 22
Fire Fighters' Concerns About Wives Safety

Interview Questions	Times Chosen (%)
49. Do you worry about your wife and family while you are on duty? **(b)**	
a. yes	62%
b. no	37%

(a) From Women's Basic Information Sheet, Appendix B
(b) From Fire Fighter's Intensive Interview, Appendix C

---

while 50% mention they discuss selected topics such as what went on at a fire, a bad rescue call or an unusual event. Sixty-seven percent of the wives agree they discuss "everything," "almost everything," or "daily activities" with their husbands (Table 23). Wives of the men who have been in the fire service for a long time and wives who are happy with their husband's work, such as Paul Jackson's wife, report feelings like this, "I think that it is very important for wives to understand the problems and the good times that our husbands go through in a job like this. I really feel that if they don't understand, a marriage can fall apart." Fjelstad (1978) concurs that marital stress decreases as identification by the fire fighter couple with the fire service increases. Finally, the fire fighters appreciate being able to talk to their wives about the job. Billy Joe Cellon reports, "With some of the problems I have, she's helped me. She's helped me come through some of the decisions I've made." The fire fighters' wives, then, are encouraged to be active listeners.

Fourth, the fire fighter wives do talk to each other about their problems and frustrations: 53.3% talk together about daily activities, the standby system with its attendant disruptions of family life, and about selected rescue calls (Table 24). It is especially important for the new wives to talk out their problems and frustrations in order for them to realize they are not alone. For example, the wife of one rookie fire fighter describes her problem, which is shared by many new fire fighters' wives: "Sometimes when you talk about worrying, impatience and loneliness appear more. When you are just married and your husband spends all day Sunday on standby transfers you get very low and

---

Table 23
Communication Between Couples About Fire Fighting

Interview Questions	Times Chosen (%)
52. What do you discuss with your wife about fire fighting? (a)	
a. Selected topics	50.0%
b. Everything	31.3%
c. Nothing	12.5%
d. Rarely talk to her about it	06.0%
49. What do you discuss with your husband about fire fighting? (b)	
a. Everything, almost everything, daily activities	66.6%
b. Not much, no answer	20.0%
c. Anything he wants to discuss, issues of general support	13.3%

(a) From Fire Fighters' Intensive Interview, Appendix C
(b) From Women's Basic Information Sheet, Appendix B

Table 24
Wives' Peer Group Support

Interview Questions	Times Chosen (%)
50. What do you discuss about fire fighting with the other wives? **(a)**	
a. Daily activities, standby system selected rescue calls	53.3%
b. Very little, not much, nothing	33.3%
c. Did not answer	13.3%
26. Would you participate in women's auxiliary if one were formed? **(a)**	
a. yes	73.3%
b. no	26.6%
41. Would you like your wife to participate in a women's auxiliary if one were formed? **(b)**	
a. yes	63.0%
b. no	37.0%

(a) From Women's Basic Information Sheet, Appendix B
(b) From Fire Fighters' Intensive Interview, Appendix C

---

downhearted." Generally, being married to a fire fighter is harder on the younger wives. The older women or those who have been married longer to fire fighters have adjusted to the irregular hours and to the disrupted family plans. They have developed support structures for themselves through family and friends, or through activities in which they participate without their husbands. The wives are expected to "adapt to continuous role changes and to cope with both the hours apart from her husband and the long hours together" (Fjelstad, 1978:77).

To enhance the wives' own cohesion and to alleviate the stress placed on individual wives, 73.3% of the women said they would join a women's auxiliary if one were formed. Further, 63%

of the men support the notion of an auxiliary. Both the women and the men view such an organization as a way for the women to formalize the activities they now do individually, such as brining food and drink to fire drills and to working fires (Table 24).

Fifth, the women's personal interest in fire fighting and the EMS system was questioned to assess their interest in and adjustment to the fire fighter occupation (Table 25). None of the women have taken a class in fire fighting, and 80% say they would not like to do so. Answers range from, "fire fighting is a man's world," and "fire fighting is too dangerous for women" to simply, "I am not interested." Thirty-eight percent of the men say they do not want their wives to take classes in fire fighting. These men consider their wives too delicate for such instruction. However, 50% responded that the choice would be left up to their wives. These men think the knowledge would enhance the women's understanding of the job. None suggested their wives become fire fighters, however.

Eighty-six percent of the women have never taken a class in emergency medicine or a paramedic class. However, 40% say they would like to take at least an EMT class. One wife, a nurse, said, "An EMT class would be handy in everyday life, but I would not be able to handle the stress of being an EMT." Another wife who had small children said, "I would like to feel I would be able to handle an emergency situation, should one arise." Most respond that they would take an EMT class to better understand their husband's job.

The fire fighters' responses are generally positive, 75% support the notion that an EMT class would be good for their wives. They consider the contents of the class to be good general knowledge for everyone and many state their wives would be better able to handle emergencies around the house with such knowledge. Fifty-six percent state they would not like their wives to have paramedic training because it would be a waste of time if such training were not going to be used professionally. Forty-four percent respond "yes" or "it is up to her" when asked if they want their wives to take a paramedic class.

Given the above data, it is perceived by both the fire fighters and their wives that the wives must understand, accept and adjust to the fire fighting occupation. Further, many of the coping mechanisms the couples use are designed to facilitate the wives' understanding of and identification with the fire service.

Table 25
Wives Interest/Involvement in Fire Fighting/Emergency Rescue

Interview Questions	Times Chosen (%)
11. Have you taken a class in FF? (a)	
a. yes	0%
b. no	100.0%
13. Would you like to take a class in FF? (a)	
a. yes	20.0%
b. no	80.0%
57. Would you like your wife to take a class in FF? (b)	
a. It's up to her	50.0%
b. no	37.5%
c. yes	12.5%
14. Have you taken a class in EMT/paramedic? (a)	
a. yes, EMT	14.0%
b. no, neither	86.0%
16. Would you like to take an EMT/paramedic class? (a)	
a. yes, EMT	40.0%
b. no, neither	60.0%
58. Would you like your wife to take an EMT/paramedic class? (b)	
a. no, EMT	25.0%
b. yes, EMT	75.0%
c. no, paramedic	56.0%
d. yes, paramedic	44.0%

(a) From Women's Basic Information Sheet, Appendix B
(b) From Fire Fighter's Intensive Interview, Appendix C

This understanding is enhanced by the fire department's acceptance of wives at station events, fire drills and working fires.

Fire Department's Role in Mitigating Family Problems

One way the wives spend more time with their husbands is through fire department sponsored activities. These formalized activities allow the women to become familiar with the men's work situation, to become familiar with some of the hazards of the occupation, and to identify more closely with a brotherhood of fire fighters. The fire chief and the men believe that family participation at these events eases the stress of long hours apart.

First, families share time through daily contact at the station. Phone calls, lunch and dinner facilitate this sharing. Often children are brought "to see daddy or 'uncle' so and so" or to "see where daddy works." Second, shift dinners occur on all major holidays to provide time for families to be together. In this way community fire protection is maintained and the family unit is solidified. Through the weekly and holiday social activities, which may be viewed as rituals, is expressed the cultural value of the family (LaFontaine, 1972:xvii).

Third, the annual Mother's Day dinner is sponsored by a local manufacturer and held at the fire station for the fire fighters and their wives or mothers. The dressy dinner is capped off by a ride on Engine 7, a 6-man pumper. The fire fighters stand behind their wives on the tailboard of the engine, or sit with them in the jump seats as the engineer on duty drives down the highway and across to the main street of Cows Crossing. It is quite a sight, with lights flashing, siren whining, the horn blaring and skirts fluttering in the wind. The ride is exhilarating and eagerly looked forward to by the women. This custom also provides the women with some insight into one of the hazards of fire fighting—riding the fire engine. It may also be interpreted as a ritual with a message about what it means to be a fire fighter.

Fourth, fire and smoke drills are a regular part of the local training program. Although they are supposed to be a surprise, the men often have advanced warning of the evening drills and arrange for their wives and children to participate from a safe distance. Eighty-seven percent of the women indicate they go to the fire drills (Table 26). Their answers vary from, "I enjoy watching my man doing what he loves," and "it is interesting to me," to "it helps me to understand him more when he's had a bad day."

Some of the women only "sit and watch from the truck," but the majority involve themselves to a much greater extent. To one woman, fire drills are "interesting and they give me some time with my fire fighter." Another said, "I watch the guys in action as much as I can and talk to the wives." One reports that "for us it's a family event. The children and I can understand more about him if we understand his job."

Sixty-nine percent of the fire fighters agree that their wives should attend the fire drills. Of these men, half think their wives' presence at a drill will enhance their understanding of fire situations. In answer to another question, 63% say they like their wives to come to a "working fire," as long as she remains out of the way (Table 26). Again, the men are interested in promoting their wives understanding of the job of fire fighting.

During the observation period, there was one fire drill which substantiates this notion that a fire drill may serve as a family event in which the wives feel a part of the action and the fire fighters feel the support of their wives and family. In August, 1978, the department had a controlled smoke drill and fire burn just outside the city limits in an old two story wood frame house.

Table 26
Wives' Interest/Involvement in Fire Fighting

Interview Questions	Times Chosen (%)
38. Do you like to go to fire drills? **(a)**	
a. yes	87%
b. no	13%
53. Do you like your wife to come to the fire drills? **(b)**	
a. yes	69%
b. no	31%
55. Do you like your wife to come to working fires? **(b)**	
a. yes	63%
b. no	37%

(a) From Women's' Basic Information Sheet, Appendix B
(b) From Fire Fighters' Intensive Interview, Appendix C

The men tested the equipment, practiced search and rescue tactics and roof rescue, as well as fire suppression tactics.

The house was located on property with a number of large trees where two streets intersected in a V. Across the wider street are two churches and there are residences and some wooded areas adjacent to the property. Both streets were blocked off by the police for the entire drill. The on-duty ambulance crew positioned itself on the wider street so that it would be available to the fire fighters or would be able to leave on other emergency runs. Older volunteer fire fighters stayed at the station in the watchroom while younger volunteers joined the paid men for the drill.

The fire fighters arrived shortly after 5 PM. As preparations began for the evolutions, both area residents and fire fighter families arrived. Wives called out to their husbands, held up the children and indicated to the men where they would be sitting during the drill. The fire fighters joined their wives for a few minutes to let them know how long the drill would take and what was going to happen. As other wives arrived, they were hailed by earlier ones, so many sat together. The men seemed genuinely happy to see their families there.

Families sat on towels or blankets along the tree belt on the church side of the street. Some brought food and nearly all brought something to drink. The wives did not cross the street during the drill; instead, the men crossed over to chat for a few minutes when they were not practicing or teaching a particular evolution.

With darkness, the fire chief signaled the end of the socializing. The house was fired with bottles of gasoline. As the flames rose higher, four-man hose teams practiced different spraying techniques. They broke windows with stones so the glass would not explode when it heated up. This was a big sport, and those who broke the glass were cheered by other fire fighters and onlookers. As the heat from the fire increased, the fire fighters' families moved back and the men turned the hoses on themselves to keep cool. The portable lights were hooked up just prior to fire suppression so that the men could do the cleanup.

During the fire suppression, there was little time for chatting between the wives and the men because everyone's attention was directed to the fire combat. Even if many of the women had seen the procedures before, few showed boredom. Children had their fathers pointed out to them often—it was difficult to distinguish the men in their protective gear. It was very exciting for the children to see their fathers and the other men involved in something as important as putting out a fire.

The fire fighter families stayed at least until the fire was out. During the cleanup, men joined their wives for brief rests and drinks. When the equipment was loaded onto the engine, some of the wives of off-duty men went to the station to wait for them to finish cleaning and reloading the engines. By 10 PM everyone had gone home or had returned to duty. The comments most often overheard from the wives were ones of happiness, pleasure at a job well-done, or expressions of interest in what they had seen.

To summarize the discussion about family problems, the fire fighters' wives have an important role in mitigating their husband's stress and in solving the problems the occupation places on their family life. As working women, they have to structure their family and social activities around the demands of the fire fighter's job and their own jobs. Together, the fire fighter couple attend fire department sponsored activities, fire drills and occasionally the women attend working fires. Proud and happy that their husbands are fire fighters, the women want to understand the job but are not interested specifically in learning the job as much as being a part of it through daily activities. Fire fighter couples agree that communication about the job, its hazards and its stress, are important to the women's understanding of the men and their occupation. Although they have no official role in the operation of the fire department, the support the women give to the men indicates they perform an important stress relieving function.

Organizational Problems/Individual Stress

The fire fighters have several specific complaints about how the fire department is operated. One hundred percent of the men suggest there are administrative problems at the station and 69% of them find the administrative problems annoying. Many of these complaints are summarized on Table 27.

First, the men object to the long hours forced on them by the 24 hour on duty, 24 hour standby system. In reality, men on standby often work 8–15 hours the day after their regular 24 hour shift because of the demand for patient transfers within and outside the county. Although they are paid for each rescue run, the money ($7.50) is not as great as each could earn at a second job. The irregular hours cut short the time the men have with their families, and wives' working schedules compound the difficulty. Further, men involved in training classes held outside the community are burdened by having to report for duty during the hours they are not in class.

Second, the gap in communication between the fire chief and the fire fighters is a sad point for many. They feel the chief is autocratic and arbitrary, particularly with regard to matters of discipline. They want a strong leader who respects them, who deals with them equitably, and who asks their opinions on management matters. Further, the chief's scheduling of station events, training classes and the station's participation in community events often coincides with the busiest season, making the men clearly overextended during the fire season.

Third, the fire fighters and the officers recognize the need for better training for the officers. The officers desire more leadership training and the men think their officers do not meet the standards they have set for a "good officer." To facilitate command, one officer and one senior fire fighter want a written delineation of each man's duties, and a formalized channel of communication so that ideas can be heard fairly. Young officers express confusion about their job and an inability to cope satisfactorily with their new status. It is hard on some of them to command a group of men with whom they were raised. For example, the assistant chief, Jack Brown, said it was a difficult adjustment for him when he was "no longer one of the boys." Also, officers do not respond to ambulance calls and some worry about their loss of rescue skills and about being isolated from "the action." Others are clearly happy about their promotions, but distressed at their sudden and relative inactivity.

Fourth, the fire fighters are concerned about their public image, which I believe is related directly to individual self-image and group cohesiveness. The men perceive the public's misuse of the ambulance service (e.g. "lizard runs"), the difficulties they occasionally encounter from hostile onlookers at rescue scenes, and the commissioners' apparent disinterest in them as evidence of low public acceptance, and poor fire fighter image in the community. The fire fighters do receive support from some parts of the community, but the recognition which means the most to the men is individualized. For example, a little girl stopped by the station one day with her parents to thank two fire fighters for their help several months earlier when she had to be transported

Table 27 Job Related Stress	
Interview Questions	Times Chosen (%)
27. Are there problems at the station?	
a. yes	100%
b. no	0%
28. What are the problems?	
a. Administration	100.%
10. What is the most annoying part of your job?	
a. Administration	68.7%
b. Lack of respect for the CCFD by the community	31.0%

to a distant hospital. The men were touched by her gifts of tomatoes and her picture, and later said that the best part of their job was knowing they had helped someone. This kind of recognition is infrequent, and the fire fighters' perceptions of their public image is poor as a result.

Ritualized Coping Processes

In a proposed pilot study dealing with the military, Hegge and Marlowe (1979) are interested in the physical and psychological demands that affect the performance readiness of soldiers. Specifically, they are interested in the stress of life threat on individuals. They raised three questions which are relevant to this research. These are: Are stress responses that are not played out within the group discharged in alternate environments, such as within the family? Are stress responses that arise externally to the group discharged within the work group? Are these displacements regularized (ritualized) or are they idiosyncratic? These questions relate to fire fighters because of the similarity between battle environments for both soldiers and fire fighters. Life threat is an occupational reality for fire fighters, who must learn to mitigate physical and emotional stress in order to function effectively as individuals and together as a unit.

First, as this research indicates, the fire fighters do take the stress of their job home, and the wives do play an important part in mitigating that stress. Also the fire department, through social events, local training sessions and through daily contact between fire fighter couples, helps alleviate family problems. Second, stress responses which arise externally to the group are the organizational problems over which they have no control. For example the men are apparently unable to influence decisions about the type and quality of the equipment they use or the pay they receive for the hours they work. This perceived lack of control over their own fate combines with the personal problems arising among the men (see below) to place added stress on men already stressed by a hazardous occupation.

Third, the present research affirms that the fire fighters do displace their stress responses in a ritualized fashion. There are two minor and two major rituals utilized by the fire fighters to mitigate the stress which arises within the work group. In general the social structure of the group is revealed by who decides if a ritual should occur, by the choice of persons to be the subject of the ritual, and by the meaning conveyed to the subject of the ritual during the ritual ceremony. A clear statement of social structure is contained in the fact that often the leaders in the ritual are senior fire fighters lead by a popular and trusted man (e.g. the "Committee"), and that the subjects of ritual are often rookie fire fighters or men who have broken the group's norms.

In addition to the socializing and disciplinary functions, the rituals reduce stress by providing the group members with a way to vent their frustration towards the norm breaker, and by providing all the fire fighters with a way to clearly state the group's norms. Stress is reduced immediately for group members after the ritual and remains at a reduced level as long as they believe all group members are adhering to the norms.

Also the leadership and discipline provided by the Committee through the rituals may be a substitute for the weak or unsatisfactory formal leadership presently at the station. The strong informal leadership developed among the men reduces stress in the group because it provides guidelines and role models for the other group members.

Two Minor Rituals: Humor and After-the-Fire Discussions

Two minor rituals are the use of humor, such as joking and practical jokes, and the formalized after-the-fire discussions. First, the fire fighters use ritual joking which facilitates communication and relieves tension. The idea of using humor to establish rapport is useful in analyzing their interpersonal relationships because the laughter which results from the humorous exchanges, in general, relieves tension between the men by releasing energy (Goodchilds, 1972:179).

Humor. On a group level, humor integrates group values of trust, teamwork and loyalty and is used in a ritualized manner to maintain group boundaries (Goodchilds, 1972:179). For example, rookie fire fighters are chosen most often as the brunt of humorous barbs and practical jokes. They are an easy target for the other men because of their inexperience in fire fighting and because it takes a few months to be oriented to the Cows Crossing station. Rookies' errors, their level of knowledge and the adjustment to fire fighter life are tested daily until they are accepted into the group. Acceptance comes with time after the new fire fighter has proved to the others that he can "take it and pay it back." Also, when the other men take the time to tease a rookie, it does indicate their willingness to accept him. For example, one rookie virtually was ignored after the men discovered that he would not respond to the kidding; he quit at the end of his three months probationary period. Ritualized joking is a constant, daily part of life at the station, and the length of time it takes for a new fire fighter to be accepted by the others depends on his personality, his ability to take the teasing, and how long he remains the newest fire fighter. When additional men are hired, the group's attention is directed to the newest rookie and away from the previous target.

Ritualized insult exchange, called ranking or verbal dueling, describes another practice used by the study group, which the fire fighters call "aggravating," "instigating," or "fuckin' with the man." The subjects the fire fighters use as a basis for the ranking process include their indicators for manliness: sexuality, personal appearance, fighting ability (Blanchette, 1979:12). The practice is used to release aggression and hierarchically to arrange the fire fighters (Goodchilds, 1972:179; Blanchette, 1979:13).

Practical jokes are another kind of humor the fire fighters constantly use to "aggravate" each other. Practical jokes take place most often during the slow months when the men have a great deal of unstructured time. These jokes are planned carefully: a fire fighter might wait days for the optimum moment to "pay back." The ideal is to wait until the subject of the joke has forgotten he had "instigated" the first round of pranks, then aggravate him when he is engaged in personal business. For example, a common prank is to pour a pitcher of ice water on a man's head while he sits on the toilet or while he is in the shower. Another joke is a variation on short-sheeting a bed: add salt to it. One man uses a particularly insidious joke if he wants to pay back the whole shift. He wears dark socks all day and the allergic reaction creates an odor so terrible that the entire barracks smells bad! Sometimes, newcomers return from an emergency run to discover their bed has been placed on top of the smoke tower or behind one of the engines. There are limits to the use of this humor, however. Nothing is to be done to a fire fighter's protective gear or to his personal vehicle. The function of humor, then, is to test a newcomer, to relieve boredom, to hierarchically arrange or rearrange the members of the group and to solidify the group.

After the fire discussion. A second minor ritual recognizes individual fire fighters for their good work, or it singles out those men who perform poorly. This ritual is the after-the-fire discussion which takes place immediately following the engine cleanup, and often is repeated over a period of weeks. As indicated by one military study, group discussions provide a vehicle for men to praise each other, and a vehicle for them to express their anxiety by exaggerating the danger or their own role in it (Bourne, 1970:96–97).

Among the fire fighters there is a group tolerance for bragging within reason. Individual acts of heroism are recognized, but not necessarily encouraged. Instead, the men know team effort is essential to their job and a feeling of *esprit de corps* is encouraged (Ulrich, 1970:12). One way to increase group solidarity is to recognize errors and to spend time discussing tactics and procedures to remedy fire suppression or rescue problems. Fifty percent of the men indicate group discussion after a fire provides an opportunity for improving their methods. These discussions indicate the group is willing to share their failures as well as their successes, and this sharing of the results of a cooperative task improves group cohesiveness (Kennedy, 1977:126).

Cooperation and group success also lead to group cohesiveness, and when members of a group are cooperatively interdependent, as is the ideal among the fire fighters, then interpersonal relations among them will improve. The men strive for cohesion, but during the after-the-fire discussions, individual fire fighters may be singled out for two reasons. First, individuals thank each other for help, an action which may smooth over previously existing grudges between the men and bring them closer to form a basis for future cooperative effort. Second, men who perform poorly are isolated for group action. Rookies' errors are excused in part because they are new. However, older fire fighters are criticized to their faces for their ineptitude, and are "watched" by the others at the next fire. Some men have difficulty in re-establishing themselves as good fire fighters. One man never was able to prove himself after a series of fire fighting errors. When these group discussions pinpoint weaknesses (e.g., persons) within the the group, they also contribute to new rounds of group dissension rather than to group cohesion, and increase the possibility of group ritual action.

Interestingly, group discussions rarely include the rookies, who are expected rather to listen and to learn fire suppression tactics and group norms. Rookies are not allowed to contribute to these conversations because they are believed to have nothing informative to contribute. If they do express their opinions, they are disregarded.

The two minor rituals, humor and group discussion, occur in response to changes in group membership and to a constant shifting relationship among the men. Changes may occur for several reasons. First, it appears to be a characteristic of individuals who are interacting to be in state of tension, and these tensions must be resolved so that group equilibrium can be maintained (Bonner, 1959:4–6). Second, changes occur when membership changes, as with the fire fighters when new men are hired. Third, some groups have a rigid structure while others are more adaptable to innovation. The fire fighters make up a relatively stable group, but their tolerance for innovation is related to the status of the innovator. Fourth, change depends on the degree of organization within the group. An organized group has higher motivation, better group participation and cooperation, interdependence and morale (Bonner, 1959:53–56, 91). The fire fighters have a weak organizational structure with poor leadership and poor morale, therefore their tolerance for innovation is reduced. One way groups handle the relationships between individuals is through ritual processes. Both the processes of joining this group of fire fighters and remaining a member of the group are marked by ritual ceremonies.

Two Major Rituals: Head Flushing and The Stretcher Treatment

The fire fighters' small group form is basic to the fire service and their members stand in more or less interdependent status with one another. The group "possessed a set of norms or values which regulated the behavior of individual members, at least in matters of consequence to the group" (Sherif, 1954:763). Further, "an individual becomes a group member to the extent that he internalizes the major norms of the group, carries on the responsibilities and meets group expectation for the position he occupies" (Sherif, 1954:763). The study group is task oriented but has some of the characteristics of an encounter group primarily because the men spend so many hours together. This close proximity among the men means they have the opportunity to learn to trust and to understand each other, and thereby to formulate a basis for the interdependence needed to be an effective team which works well under pressure. Norm breakers and innovators are regarded with suspicion because they threaten the cohesion and interdependence the fire fighters must maintain in order to remain an effective functioning team. Ritual action may be used to redress the actions taken by the norm breakers. Both Turner (1968:279) and Leaf (1974:157–158) perceive rituals as having a message or serving as message transmitters from the group to the individual.

Two specific rituals form one of the most fascinating parts of the research. One is called "head flushing" or "becoming an 'episscopalian'" (sic), and the other one is called "the stretcher treatment." Each ritual has a prescribed set of symbols used in different combinations. The motives of the men who carry out the ritual and the effect on the initiate differ with each incident. The important thing to remember is that these rituals are initiated by the men through instigation by the Committee. The officers know about them; many officers have had their heads flushed. However, when a man becomes an officer he is allowed only to observe the stretcher treatment. One exception to this rule occurred during the observation period when a captain was put on the stretcher before he got married.

Head flushing. Head flushing is a "tradition" which began around 1972. It happens to everyone, but especially to rookies and to men who say it cannot happen to them. Brad Whitehurst reports that when he joined the CCFD he knew that most fire departments had rituals, but "this is about the most drastic one I've heard of. By the time I first heard about head flushing, I was on my way over there [to the urinal]."

The ritual involves usually five or six men, one of whom is the "flushee." The initiate is grabbed, turned on his back and carried to the barracks urinal. Onlookers cheer and call encouragement to the participants. If the initiate struggles, the participants seem to enjoy the ritual more. Once in the bathroom, his head is placed under the running water and the urinal is flushed by as many as wish to participate. The initiate is dropped to the floor and left alone for a few minutes to work out any anger he may be feeling. When he comes out of the bathroom, the others expect him to smile and take the process good naturedly. If he does not, they may repeat the process immediately "to show him we can do other things." The fire fighters said the urinal water symbolizes the water used by them.

The reasons for the initial appearance of head flushing is not clear in anyone's mind. However, a consensus of opinion is as Billy Joe Cellon says, "a welcome to the club. You're a part of the family, you're one of the gang. It is nothing against anybody, it's really a compliment. It's an acceptance." When used in this sense the head flushing is a rite of passage such as those van Gennep (1960) describes.

Van Gennep's three stages of ritual apply to the fire fighter who is separated through training and group socialization from previous ties or identities with other occupational groups. The transitional stage, the ritual itself, may occur anytime after the fire fighter has been hired, although it usually occurs within the first month. Acceptance into the family of fire fighters is based partly on the ritual, how well the rookie takes the ritual and on how well the rookie is doing generally as a fire fighter.

The ritual is also called "becoming an 'epissscopalian'" (sic). Tommy Lee reports, "I don't know where it originated. When I came down here I was told I'd become an Episcopalian. I didn't know exactly what that meant at the time because I'm a Methodist. Found out real quick the night all the guys showed up on their night off." Tommy is 6'3" and weighs well over 200 pounds; it apparently took nearly all the men to carry him to the urinal.

One variation in the head flushing occurred when Johnny Butter, another large and very strong fire fighter, refused to allow the others to carry him to the barracks. He locked his arms around the rail on the tailboard of Engine 7. Twelve men tried to pry him loose, but could not. Their solution was to bring the garden hose to where he stood and "wet him."

As time went on, any man who was promoted, finished a class or who's wife had a baby had his head flushed to prevent "him getting a swelled head." When the ritual is done with this interpretation, it is a rite of intensification designed to restore group equilibrium by changing the individual's attitude to be more in line with those of the other group members (Chapple, 1942:). The ritual occurs so frequently that most men have lost count as to the number of times each "has been to the toilet." Paul Jackson observed, "It seems like every time you get a promotion, or get a certificate, or pass a test with the fire department, they politely flush your head. I think at last count, I've had my head flushed about twenty times." The ritual process has evolved to the point that a man may have his head flushed at the whim of any other man. Joe Smith maintains, "Mostly we do it 'cuz we're bored." The only requirement in this case is getting enough other fire fighters to carry the subject to the urinal.

This ritual process largely serves as an initiation. Head flushing provides a means by which the group can change its attitude towards the rookie; they can treat him as a member of the group rather than as an outsider (Turner, 1969:201–203). The ritual also serves as a break in the monotony, as a test to see if a man can take a joke, or even as a "payback" for a practical joke. All the respondents state the ritual is not designed to hurt anyone, however, no one mentioned liking having it done to him.

Stretcher treatment. In his discussion of initiations and secret societies, Tiger points out that initiations are "frequently bizarre, often cruel and of profound significance to both members and aspirants" (1969:110). Further, these aspects of ritual "suggest the importance of initiation and the exclusivist and selective principles it functions to defend" (Tiger, 1969:110). He posits that initiation ceremonies "symbolize a concern men have with the qualities of courage, competence and loyalty" (Tiger, 1969:143). A group "we-feeling" is established or re-established partially through shared ritual processes.

The stretcher treatment is the fourth ritual, the most complex and the harshest treatment the fire fighters give to each other. Initially, the men believe the stretcher treatment symbolized the medical side of their dual occupation. Not all the fire fighters have been on the stretcher. Rather, it is reserved as a way to redress what the men perceive to be an "attitude problem," or it is perceived as "playing" when done to a man about to be married.

The thought of being placed on the stretcher elicits defensive reactions on the part of some potential candidates. For example, at coffee one morning, it was rumored that Bobby T. had gotten engaged over the weekend, so the others on his shift spontaneously decided to put him on the stretcher. I observed five men run from the kitchen to the parking lot where the "engaged" man stood. He saw his shift mates coming toward him and drew his knife. He was circled immediately by the men who had drawn their knives in response. When it was determined that he was not engaged after all, the knives were pocketed quickly.

Normally, the stretcher treatment is planned carefully and calculatedly. The Committee is in charge of initiating rituals of redress to cure an attitude problem and to re-establish group solidarity. It is an *ad hoc* group of five or six senior fire fighters, most of whom have grown up together in Cows Crossing. The president is Joe Smith, who is also a key informant, and the vice president is his friend, Bobby T. Tomlinson. These men are looked to by the others to plan the ritual process. Officers may serve as "consultants to the Committee," as Bobby T. did when he was promoted to officer rank, but may not be a part of the ritual except to watch. In this way the officers are aware of the ritual processes and in some cases fully approve of the men's actions. However, the men believe that their awareness and presence at the ritual also assures that "no real harm" comes to the subject of the ceremony.

As mentioned above, the men must be able to work as a team and the team must agree on just how they will work together. This teamwork is developed through formal training and by the development of a group code of ethics or norms. "Attitude problems" are men who just do not fit into the group. Perhaps they too often suggest changes in fire fighting tactics or in administrative procedures. Such a person is described variously as "a know it all," "someone who does not do his share of the work," "someone who doesn't care about his profession," or someone who is in another way perceived as untrustworthy or a threat to group solidarity.

"J.W." Jones says.

> An attitude problem is when someone fails to change his ways or modify his ways so that he falls into the mainstream of what's actually going on at the fire station. Everybody has to get together and think along the same track at least in the fire house.

Problems reportedly need to be corrected before group solidarity is broken or before the attitude problems damage the professional image of the fire fighters. "Attitude problems" create stress among the other men.

With regard to the stretcher treatment, Paul Jackson said it started "because a couple of guys had bad attitudes that needed straightening out. If it doesn't work, you do it again." Brad Whitehurst describes the treatment as "the tool of the governing agency within the department to issue reprimands that don't come from the chief."

The stretcher treatment occurs usually in the late afternoon or early evening during the warmer months of the year. Before the ritual begins, a man is told by the president of the Committee why he will be "put on the stretcher" and is given the option of going on with or without a struggle. There are always enough fire fighters around to ensure no escape. Not everyone participates to the same degree: those who do not wholeheartedly approve of the ritual only watch, while others do things which they believe will not really harm the initiate, like call out encouragement or instructions to the others. After being stripped naked or just to his shorts, he is taped to the stretcher. Sometimes a man's eyes and mouth are taped also. Various greases, creams or paints are applied to his body: axle grease, shaving cream, food coloring or spray paint are some of the products used. Sometimes a man has his chest hair shaved or his initials shaved into it. Others have their pubic hair or both chest and pubic hair shaved. Sometimes a man's penis is painted with spray paint or gension violet. Products are chosen, apparently, for their lasting value (Illustration 1).

The man is left on median of the four lane highway adjacent to the fire department, or is placed at the edge of a side street or in the bay of the station. In any case, he has to get off

Illustration 1
The Stretcher Treatment

the stretcher without assistance, a process which may take several minutes. The others watch the initiate until he has returned to the station. Usually more than an hour is spent trying to remove the grease and the paint, some of the paint has to wear off. For several hours after that, Joe Smith reports, "the man is left alone to work things over in his mind."

Men who are given the stretcher treatment decide either to adhere to group norms or they resign from the station. "The member's motivation to perform the normative behavior will be greatly affected by his dependence on the group: to the degree that the group can give him what he wants [e.g., status or acceptance], he will be likely to conform" (Thibault, 1959:255). The individual has to decide how badly he wants to be a fire fighter at that station and how much group acceptance means to him.

Opinions on the use of the stretcher treatment vary among the fire fighters. Brad Whitehurst reiterated what another man said,

> The guys down here use the stretcher treatment for intradepartment reprimands. I don't agree with the stretcher, but I agree with the principle behind it: that every department of this size or bigger needs a governing agency inside it that nobody else knows about. That has a tendency to keep everyone in line. Besides, the chief doesn't want to hear about all the problems between the men, so the men take of it.

Not all the men have been on the stretcher, although in Sam Turner's case, he has been on it three times in three years. Bobby T. Tomlinson has been on it seven times in seven years, but reports, "they was just playing with me." The stretcher treatment is not meant to hurt anyone, but is variously described as a way to "humiliate a man," to "straighten him out" or to "show him that we could do other things." However, some men have been injured physically, including the participants as well as the initiate, and Ron Emmet reports that he was "freaked out" by the experience. Also, about this latter case, Joe said, "We have never intentionally hurt anyone at any time. Apparently we went too far and we screwed up his mind. We meant only to make an impression on him. We didn't really do anything that bad and for about three weeks he didn't have nothing to say. He just did his work."

The frequency of the ritual stretcher treatment does not occur within any regular measurable span of time. The ritual occurs on an *ad hoc* basis whenever the group, or specifically the Committee, decides there is a perceptible chink in the group's solidarity. Two or three men may be subjected to the stretcher treatment in a short period of time (2–4 months), then no one else may be put on the stretcher for several months.

This ritual process snowballed until Ron Emmet threatened to knife the others if they tried to put him on the stretcher again. After this incident, many fire fighters stated it had gone too far, and the assistant chief, Jack Brown, stated he would prohibit both major rituals if the chief would support him. Jack was interviewed shortly after he took his leave of absence and was told about a recurrence of the stretcher treatment. He said,

> I don't agree with any of it. Somebody is going to get hurt in the end. A lot of people can take it as a joke one time, not two times. Shaving someone! You're kidding! Somebody is going to get hurt . . . heaven forbid, you start fooling around with a razor like that. I don't think it would be hard to make them stop doing it. They know I wouldn't have to give them an ultimatum, but they know I would do something if it [the order to stop] wasn't obeyed. I think most of them would go along with it because I don't think they really like it that much. What's happened, it's like a snowball, kept building.

Prohibition from the officers is probably the only way the men will stop performing this ritual. The men who do not approve of the ritual participate in some way, even if it is only to watch, because they believe if they try to prevent the stretcher treatment they will be the next victim.

In relating the ritual to stress and group behavior, du Toit's (1979) model once again is useful (Diagram 2). The crisis for the members of the group lies in one member's reluctance to accept the group norms. Group members meet to discuss the action to be taken: if the norm breaker accepts their initial criticism of him and adjusts his behavior, individual anxiety is reduced within the group and there is no further action required. If the norm breaker persists in his unacceptable behavior, then ritual action is decided upon. The result of the ritual action for the individual is three-fold: he may elect to resign from the fire department; he may accept the group norms and adjust his behavior; or he may not accept the norms, in which case the group may elect to repeat the ritual. The stress of the other individuals within the

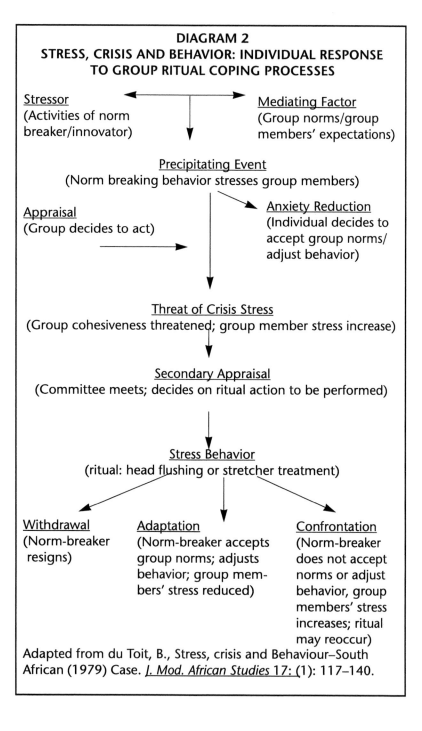

DIAGRAM 2
STRESS, CRISIS AND BEHAVIOR: INDIVIDUAL RESPONSE
TO GROUP RITUAL COPING PROCESSES

Stressor
(Activities of norm
breaker/innovator)

Mediating Factor
(Group norms/group
members' expectations)

Precipitating Event
(Norm breaking behavior stresses group members)

Appraisal
(Group decides to act)

Anxiety Reduction
(Individual decides to
accept group norms/
adjust behavior)

Threat of Crisis Stress
(Group cohesiveness threatened; group member stress increase)

Secondary Appraisal
(Committee meets; decides on ritual action to be performed)

Stress Behavior
(ritual: head flushing or stretcher treatment)

Withdrawal
(Norm-breaker
resigns)

Adaptation
(Norm-breaker accepts
group norms; adjusts
behavior; group mem-
bers' stress reduced)

Confrontation
(Norm-breaker
does not accept
norms or adjust
behavior, group
members' stress
increases; ritual
may reoccur)

Adapted from du Toit, B., Stress, crisis and Behaviour–South
African (1979) Case. *J. Mod. African Studies* 17: (1): 117–140.

group is relieved only when the norm breaker either resigns or accepts group norms.

In a small group, the function of a ritual is to restore the right relationship between two people or to restore the relations between an individual and the group (Turner, 1969:201–202). Rituals of status elevation and rituals of status reversal reinforce the social structure of the group (Turner, 1969:201). The ritual processes also function as communication systems in which the initiate clearly is given a message from the group (Leaf, 1974:157–158). Among the fire fighters, rituals are perceived to restore relationships among the members and function as a clear message to group members.

In summary, in the case of the two major rituals used by the fire fighters, the meaning assigned to the ritual varies with the subject of the ritual and the reasons for utilizing the ritual process. Head flushing is considered a ritual of status elevation when a man first joins the department or completes some phase of training. The same ritual is considered a ritual of status reversal when done to an officer. It is a ritual of redress when done with the belief that one fire fighter is elevating himself above the others, or it may be used to take care of a small attitude problem.

With the stretcher treatment, the fire fighters' group attitude is playful when any engaged man is placed on the stretcher. For an individual participant, this may be an opportunity to "pay back the person who receives the stretcher treatment." However, when the stretcher treatment is used as a ritual of redress, the clear implication is that the subject of the process is being reprimanded by the group. He is considered to be out of step with the rest of the fire fighters, and the authority of the group or its norms are invoked to get the errant fire fighter back in line. Group solidarity is returned to normal some time after the ritual—when the individual who was redressed indicates a willingness to accept and internalize group norms.

By using rituals of redress, a message is transmitted by the fire fighters to the subject of the ritual about his behavior and about the group's expectations for a change in his behavior. Actual change in the individual's behavior indicates to the group that their message has been received and acted upon. Finally, a change in the behavior of the subject allows the group to change its attitude or behavior towards the individual: the result of the ritual is to allow the group to be unified.

8

CONCLUSIONS

What follows includes a restatement of the hypotheses with conclusions which wholly or partially substantiate them; a statement of where the present research fits into anthropology; a set of propositions which suggest how this research may be used in future anthropological studies or as a database for studies by other social scientists; and a list of changes which may be incorporated by the Cows Crossing Fire Department to achieve the cohesiveness the fire fighters' desire.

The fire fighters' group structure is a paramilitary one in which the men are ranked and have duties and responsibilities attached to each rank. However, either these duties are not written down and delineated clearly to the men, or the men are not supervised in the manner many of them think is necessary. There are many complaints about men who do not do their share of the work or who do it poorly. Also channels of communication are supposed to follow a military pattern from fire fighter to shift captain to assistant chief to the chief, who is then to represent them to the community. In fact, the lines of communication are open and free only between the fire fighters and the assistant chief. Communication lines are broken between the chief and his officers and between the chief and the commissioners. The result is that fire fighters believe their ideas are not given a fair hearing and that they are not well represented to the commissioners.

Order and discipline are supposed to be imposed on the fire fighters by the chief through the assistant chief and his shift captains. However, the daily operation of the station is left to the captains with the chief intervening only when his orders are not carried out or when a disciplinary action is necessary. Discipline is arbitrary and inequitable.

The fire fighters and the shift captains perceive the officers to be poorly trained in administration and field command, and agree the officers need more training. Most fire fighters think the chief should be replaced with a strong leader, who will respect and trust them as well as treat them equitably in disciplinary matters. The paramilitary system provides the latitude for a strong leader to develop, and provides a means for clear channels of communication among fire fighters, officers, the chief and the community. Instead, there exists within their paramilitary structure, an informal social structure which often wields greater authority than does the formal system. The fire fighters organize themselves by assigning high status to senior fire fighters based on characteristics such as fire fighting capability, trust, dedication to the job and the internalization of group norms. One small group of senior fire fighters compose the Committee which reprimands other fire fighters consistently, but more severely, than does the fire chief. Rookie fire fighters have the lowest status and are accepted as members of the group only after the others have worked with them and have developed a bond of trust with them.

The Cows Crossing fire fighters are dissatisfied primarily because of the problems generated by the present interpretation of how a paramilitary system should operate. They have little individual autonomy, are unable to change the rules of the formal organization, and are led by an arbitrary and paternalistic man whose own ideas of fire fighter image and professionalism do not coincide with the men's. The men have shared training and job experiences, however, and it is with these that they identify the members of their group. Further, the solidarity which develops among the fire fighters forms the basis for a team effort between the fire fighters and other subsystems within the community to provide emergency medical care, fire protection and disaster preparedness.

The fire fighters use a system of graduated rituals which allows the acceptance of newcomers, assigns roles and statuses to all the fire fighters, and which redresses errors made against group norms. The rituals relieve individual stress and promote group solidarity. The fire fighters believe their paramilitary structure is too lenient primarily because of the unresolved administrative problems, which include the inability or unwillingness of the officers to lead the men as a disciplined group assigned to a hazardous occupation. However, until a strong leader is developed, the men are determined to continue using their ritual coping mechanisms to maintain group solidarity, to maintain group discipline and image, and to maintain group boundaries through adherence to group norms.

Substantiation of Hypotheses

This research is designed to describe the job of fire fighting as interpreted by one group of fire fighters in a rural southern station. Further, the research examines the intragroup structure, which includes an elucidation of group norms, cohesiveness, attitudes and value systems, as well as the function of ritual coping processes used to relieve stress and to maintain group solidarity. One question raised at this point concerns the research objectives: "What did the research show about the function of ritual processes among the study group relative to their social structure/group cohesiveness?" There are four interrelated hypotheses generated to fulfill the research objectives. Three of the hypotheses are substantiated by the research, while the fourth is substantiated only partially.

First, group cohesiveness is fostered by rigorous, specialized training which emphasizes technical expertise, confidence and teamwork. Priorities for the fire fighters include a desire for advanced training and dedication to making fire fighting more professional. The formal training includes a constant emphasis on teamwork, the strength of the buddy system in fire fighting and fire rescue, and a de-emphasis on "heroism." The emphasis placed on advanced training, certification and willingness to work are part of the code of ethics or group norms to which both fire fighters and officers adhere. Finally, the comradeship which develops during training helps create a cohesive functioning unit which then works effectively in actual fire combat.

The second hypothesis is substantiated because group cohesiveness is fostered by informal socialization rituals practiced on the job. Informal socialization rituals are utilized as a means of enforcing group norms. The minor rituals are used specifically to accept newcomers and to remind individuals that they are part of a group and always must consider themselves part of a team effort. The major rituals are used specifically to redress errors made by norm breakers or innovators. The function of the two major rituals is to alter somehow the behavior of the entire group. With head flushing, group attitudes towards the initiate change as he is incorporated into the group structure; it functions as a rite of passage. With the stretcher treatment, the group tries to change an individual's attitudes to be more in line with those of the group norms; it functions as a ritual of redress. In all instances of ritual use, the group is giving a message to the individual: senior fire fighters do the ritual and are influential in other aspects of fire fighting; rookie fire fighters, norm breakers and innovators are in a relatively weaker position; and to remain a fire fighter at that station, one must subscribe to the group norms.

Ritual processes foster group cohesiveness even though some individuals disagree with the application of some of the rituals. Those who disagree still subscribe to the group belief that discipline and reprimands are necessary and that at this station, a self-regulating agency among the men is necessary for group cohesiveness.

Third, group cohesiveness reflects community standards and shared attitudes about family, social class and ethnic group. Family is important to the men, although the occupation of fire fighting may have greater priority in their lives. The fire fighters are intensely involved in the training and daily activities of their job and much of their energy is directed to performing firefighting tasks properly. Adjustment to the occupation by the fire fighter couple rests largely on the wife. Both wives and fire fighters agree that the wife will understand her fire fighter if she understands the job. This understanding comes through her participation in and observation of the daily life at the station, of fire drills, or of actual fires. Her further support is encouraged by the notion of a women's auxiliary and through the men's support for the women's training in emergency medicine and fire fighting. The fire fighters are family men who appreciate an occupational structure which allows their families to participate in their careers.

The fire fighters make up a homogeneous group of working class males who recognize their social class standing and who prefer the company of males during work and leisure hours. They are white Southerners who prefer not to integrate their work team ethnically or sexually.

The fourth hypothesis is partially substantiated. Group cohesiveness does enhance the effectiveness of the fire fighting/emergency rescue operations. The small group is basic to fire fighting and without a buddy system and team effort, saving lives and property would be hampered greatly. They continually emphasize teamwork through formal training and informal socialization processes. Through the use of humor and group discussion about tactics and teamwork, the fire fighters share the happiness of their successes and the sadness of their failures resulting in heightened group solidarity. The fire fighters consider themselves an effective team and praise individuals for their effort. However, they also recognize their weaknesses and are willing to take action to correct those weaknesses.

Group cohesiveness may also detract from group effectiveness if the fire fighters are so bound by their group norms that they are unable to work effectively and interdependently with other groups. However, the fire fighters do cooperate with the police, other fire departments and the hospital emergency room staff during both disaster preparedness drills and during actual emergencies. Therefore, the fire fighters' recognition that the team effort of several groups is necessary to meet large scale disasters apparently is more powerful than their emphasis on intra-group cohesiveness. In contrast, while teamwork presupposes that group cohesiveness is established through formal training, and presupposes that teamwork enhances group cohesiveness, teamwork may also lay the groundwork for group dysfunction. That is, by having to work in teams, the men are given an opportunity to evaluate and praise the capable fire fighters, and they are given the opportunity to evaluate and isolate the poor performing fire fighters. In this instance, teamwork detracts from group cohesiveness and perceived fire fighter effectiveness.

A central cluster of conclusions revolves around one question: "Are the Cows Crossing fire fighters a cohesive unit, or are they a group of disparate individuals simply hired to do the same job?" The answer is both yes, they are a cohesive unit, and no, they are not cohesive.

Cohesiveness may include the four aspects of cooperation, democratic leadership, the existence of a previous organization within the group, and membership in a persistently high status group, and may include the notion that in order to perform rituals a group has to be a cohesive unit. The fire fighters manifest only some of these aspects of cohesiveness.

First, the fire fighters as a whole do cooperate in the performance of their duties and they do cooperate in the performance of rituals. Second, the paramilitary structure provides latitude for the development of one of several types of leadership. The fire fighters have authoritarian leader with whom they are not satisfied. However, democratic leadership is not perceived by them as necessary for group cohesiveness. Instead, they prefer a strong leader who will solicit their opinions, implement their ideas, but who will take responsibility for the decisions himself. Finally, the fire fighters do not belong to a high status group within the community, but are relegated to a working class position and are considered public servants.

One way to fully answer the question of cohesiveness is to view the fire fighters as a dynamic group which endures changes in membership, changes in training, and changes in the hazards of their job. Also the stress individuals face, the stress individuals take home to their families and bring back from their families, and the stress individuals resolve through group ritual together contribute to the dynamic quality of the group. The group appears to range in and out of cohesiveness. Or, perhaps, they are in the process of becoming cohesive, or are hanging onto or redefining a previously existing cohesiveness. The take over by a group of senior fire fighters certainly is evidence of an attempt to retain cohesion. The men are cohesive enough to do their job, to identify themselves as fire fighters and to recognize others of the group as good fire fighters. However, they are not as cohesive a unit as they wish to become.

Where This Research Fits Into Anthropology

As indicated in the theoretical statement I am influenced by Radcliffe-Brown's writings on functionalism and by Victor Turner's use of functionalism to discuss the role of ritual processes to maintain group solidarity. Although the research is largely descriptive in order to present an ethnographic understanding of the perceptions the fire fighters share, the functionalist approach is the key to the analytic framework. With the functionalist approach the research demonstrates the role of ritual processes *vis a vis* social solidarity by looking at its affect upon individual group members. The ritual process provides individuals with the choice of either internalizing group norms and allowing themselves to be placed in the social structure, or resigning from the station. To the extent that the research describes the use of ritual processes in the social life of the fire fighters, it is an extension of Radcliffe-Brown's functionalism.

Although several ritual processes are discussed in this research, the study focuses on one, the stretcher treatment, which is largely an extension of Turner's eight point discussion of the rituals of redress. First, social solidarity is at least temporarily the product of ritual processes. Second, the rituals evolve out of the group's desire for cohesiveness. Nearly all the fire fighters attend the rituals of redress and even though there are differences of opinion among the men, they uniformly wish to overcome those differences and create a more unified group. Third, the data substantiate Turner's assumption that to perform ritual ceremonies, a group has to be somewhat cohesive. Fourth, the ritual processes and particularly the ritual of redress, are concerned with regaining a balance within the group, which is maintained if all the fire fighters agree to uphold the group norms. Fifth, the individual fire fighter who is the subject of ritual is informed through the ritual process that he should subordinate his desires to his assigned role and status within the group. After a fire fighter has attained a certain rank or status, then he may be heard more favorably and may effect some changes in the organization. Sixth, the reward for individual subordination is the trust and cooperation of the other men. Seventh, the aim of the ritual is to encourage the individual to accept the group norms so that a balance of relations can be maintained. The research on the fire fighters' use of ritual processes substantiates Turner's assertion that rituals of redress do not anticipate strains and tensions within a group, but are designed to correct them once they have begun to impair seriously the orderly functioning of the group.

Finally, several fire fighters agree with Turner's definition of just what processes are rituals of redress. Seven men resigned from the CCFD within 18 months after the conclusion of the observation period: four went to other fire departments in the South, while the other three took non-fire related jobs. The field data and intensive interviews suggest that four men quit in part because they believe the stretcher treatment is used against men who have innovative suggestions. This substantiates the assertion that both norm breakers and innovators may be subject to redress because the group social structure cannot tolerate the strain which results from the activities of either.

Future Social Science Studies

The data serve as a base for future comparative research in small groups. One suggestion is to study rural, paid fire departments across the nation on a cultural region basis. For instance, another anthropologist might study five rural fire departments in each region and use the data to generalize to the fire service throughout the country. In this way organizational problems, family problems and problems with stress can be pinpointed, and preventive measures can be instituted through fire fighter training programs.

Alternatively, paid fire departments can be compared and contrasted to volunteer departments. Volunteers make up the clear majority of fire fighters in America, but the scene is changing with the continued impact of urbanization and industrialization. By comparing volunteer and paid departments, a continuum of change can be predicted. Again, technical training, and organizational problems which fire departments face in a change-over from volunteer to paid status could be identified and resolved. Certainly, such large scale studies would be relevant in the United States where fire fighters occupy a hazardous job, where arson is on an increase, and where hazardous materials incidents occur more frequently. It may well be that the job of fire fighting—with its hazards, stress and need for skilled workers—will become the standard to which studies of other small work groups are compared.

The present study also serves as a database for several focused social science studies within the fire service such as ergonomic and nutrition assessments, personality inventories, as well as stress analysis and the mitigation of stress. Ideally, an interdisciplinary approach would include contributions from physical anthropologists, sociologists and social psychologists. Such an interdisciplinary approach could address issues of energy output and nutritional intake, a health assessment relative to job requirements, workers under stress and stress reduction, and the integration of these data into fire fighter training programs.

The current research does not specify how the informal leaders came into power, nor what personal gratification they receive from establishing group norms and initiating group ritual. Their emergence as leaders could be examined through the identification of dyads and triads within the group. Of interest, then, are the personal power plays within the group.

Related to the above are questions of differences in personality of individual fire fighters. The current research does not address questions about who, or what type of personality, makes a good fire fighter, who makes a good team member and who is likely to participate in rituals which maintain the group norms. This last is interesting because there are fire fighters who do not approve of the ritual processes. Why did not these non-approvers unite and prevent the rituals, or institute less drastic ones? Is it only a fear of reprisal from the group which prevents them from doing so?

The material on individual and family stress forms a basis for more focused research on how the men vent their frustrations at home. The current research does not answer specific questions about coping mechanisms which may include drugs, alcohol or spouse abuse. The question of psychosomatic illnesses resulting from stress are not addressed by the present research. Therefore, long range research on the biological effects of prolonged stress would be of use to the fire service, by fire fighter families, or as comparative material for use by biological and social scientists. Also a closer examination of family problems might answer questions about leadership roles shared or not shared between the fire fighters and their wives. For instance, after several hours (days) away from home, does the fire fighter resume his role as head of the family or are these working class families more egalitarian than has been presumed about other occupational groups within the working class?

Also questions about the relationship between the father and his children bears examination. Do the children idolize their father, or how does his absence affect them in other ways? Answers to these questions have particular relevance to forest fire fighters, who often must leave their homes for weeks at a time. Finally, the answers to the questions posed above may be relevant to groups of males attached to other service oriented occupations such as the police, railroaders, prison guards, forest logging crews or crews assigned to oil rigs in the ocean.

Proposed Changes Within the Structure of the CCFD

The first step in making the current research relevant to other social scientists is to use it to develop proposals for positive changes within the study group. The fire service itself is concerned about departmental management and recognizes the place for small group study within its ranks. They are concerned about stress, burnout and their mitigation. They are concerned about maintaining group effectiveness among men who must work closely under hazardous conditions. The fire fighters of Cows Crossing also recognize the need for change. Their suggestions are included in the field data and are presented below by category: administrative changes, stress release suggestions, and fire fighter image.

Administrative

The administration at the station drew the largest number of complaints, and the most well thought out suggestions for change. The fire fighters want to replace their chief with a strong leader, who will find out what the men want, and represent them fairly to the commissioners. Such a leader would obviate the occasionally perceived need for a union.

The men want to replace the seniority system with a promotion through testing system, which they believe is a more equitable method for advancement. Presumably the more capable fire fighters would advance quickly and there would be lower levels of frustration among those capable fire fighters who otherwise remain in an inferior position in the department. A parallel reward system of pay incentives, awards for longevity or merit could be initiated for good fire fighters who are not officer material.

The department needs six more fire fighters, two on each shift, to eliminate the need for a standby system, which is a major source of physical and emotional stress within the department. Restructuring the work schedule would save money which the commissioners now pay to fire fighters for individual runs made on standby days. A 24 hours on duty, 48 hours off duty system would provide each man with adequate rest away from the station, and would provide enough time for the men to hold second jobs.

The volunteers need to be integrated more completely into the fire fighting system. Those who can no longer function at a fire should be retired and replaced with younger men, who are well-trained, dedicated to fire fighting and who are willing to work with the paid men. The fire fighters suggest this integration would add to the professionalism of the department and to the department's status within the community.

Stress Release

Certain kinds of stress the fire fighters feel would be mitigated by the above organizational/administrative changes. However, there are some specific suggestions which might further relieve individual stress. The stress of inactivity could be mitigated by a structured work day which includes a physical fitness program, regular weekly classroom training, drills and facility cleanup. Men should be scheduled to attend classes, seminars and demonstrations throughout the year, not just during the fire season when they are forced to deal with an increased work load.

The release of emotional stress is essential to individual effective functioning. One way to release this specific kind of stress or to mitigate the physical burden of the specific and intense activities involved in fire suppression, would be to institute a regular physical fitness program. The fire fighters could be taught other stress release procedures such as training in "talking out" their fears and frustrations, or changes in diet or changes in smoking habits.

Family problems could be mitigated in part if the wives had a publicly recognized function within the fire department. A majority of the women suggested an auxiliary be formed in which they officially could do as a group what individuals already do: bring food and drinks to working fires and give each other moral support. Also an auxiliary could orient new wives to fire fighting and to the Cows Crossing Fire Department. Finally, an auxiliary would be a way for the wives to become acquainted with the occupation of fire fighting and there by increase their understanding and identification with the fire service.

For their own protection and to maintain control in an emergency situation, the fire fighters need to learn to deal more effectively with hostile onlookers and combative patients. The urgency of their work does not always provide the time for "playing psychiatrist" and many of the men would be more effective rescuers if they knew how to "cool out" situations or how to calm hysterical patients. Also a good bedside manner would enhance their self-image as well as their public image.

Fire Fighter Image

Self-esteem is very important particularly to public service employees who are constantly on display in their own community as they attend drills, fires and non-fire related emergencies. Constant observation can be stressful. In response, the fire fighters look to their own group for confirmation that what they do is correct and valuable. Morale would be improved significantly if there were publicly recognized rewards for good work, outstanding effort, a special rescue and so forth. Such a reward system would enhance the present system of promotion and the certification they receive from various training centers. Also their self image would be enhanced if they believed the commissioners thought they were worth the expenditure for new protective gear and breathing apparatus, as well as for new engines and an additional rescue vehicle.

Finally, the fire fighters' public image could be improved by developing the lieutenant's position into a fire prevention/fire education position with public relations overtones. Through this office the fire fighters could get feedback from the community: areas of strength could be enhanced and weaknesses could be corrected.

These suggestions made by the men are consistent with the latitude inherent in a paramilitary system. They are made to provide a more workable system in which individual fire fighters could advance and the group could have a more structurally sound basis for cohesiveness. In addition, their self-image as professional men dedicated to saving lives and property through discipline, hard work and team effort would be enhanced.

———◆———

REFERENCES

Ablon, J. (1977). Field methods in working with middle-class Americans: New issues of values, personality and reciprocity. Human Organization, 36 (1), 69–72.

Adams, R. N. & Preiss, J. J. (Eds.) (1960). Human organization research: Field relations and techniques. Homewood, IL: Dorsey Press.

Albert, C., Cargill-Mazer, K., Federman, D., Fell, P., Franco, R., & Gibbs, T. (1977). An evolution of an experiment in health care in rural Alachua County. Unpublished manuscript, University of Florida, Gainesville, FL.

Arensburg, C. & Kimball, S. (1965). Culture and community. New York: Harcourt, Brace and World, Inc.

Aries, E. (1977). Male-female interpersonal styles in all male, all female and mixed groups. In A. G. Sargeant (Ed.), Beyond sex roles (pp. 292–299). St. Paul, MN: West Publishing Co.

Barth, F. (1969). Ethnic groups and boundaries. Oslo, Norway: Johansen and Nielson Boktrykkeri.

Becker, H. S. & Geer, B. (1957). Participant observation and interviewing: A rejoinder. Human Organization, 16 (3), 39–40.

Becker, H. S., Geer, B., Reismon, D., & Weiss, R. S. (1968). Institutions and the person. Chicago, IL: Aldine Publishers.

Bennis, W. G., & Shephard, H. A. (1970). Group observation. In T. M. Mills and M. J. Rosenberg (Eds.), Readings on the sociology of small groups (pp. 118–128). Englewood Cliffs, NJ: Prentice Hall Publishers.

Bernard, H. R., & Lozier, J. (1973) A survey of knowledge and attitudes toward fire protection and prevention in rural Marion, Monongalia and Preston Counties, West Virginia. Unpublished manuscript, West Virginia University, Morgantown, W. Virginia.

Blanchette, R. (1978). Ranking: A study of verbal insult. The Florida Journal of Anthropology, 4 (1), 11–24.

Bonner, H. (1959). Group dynamics. New York: Ronald Press Co.

Bourne, P.G. (1970). Men, stress and Vietnam. Boston, MA: Little, Brown and Co.

Brana-Shute, G. (1974). Street corner *winkels* and dispersed households: Male adaptation to marginality in a lower class Creole neighborhood in Paramaribo. Doctoral dissertation, University of Florida, Gainesville, FL.

Brana-Shute, G. (1978). On the corner: Male social life in a Paramaribo Creole neighborhood. The Netherlands: Van Grocum and Co.

Brim, J. A. & Spain, D. H. (1974). Research design in anthropology: Paradigms and pragmatics in the testing of hypotheses. New York: Holt, Rinehart & Winston.

Bruyn, S. (1963). The methodology of participant observation. Human Organization, 22, (2), 224–235.

Bryan, J. L. (1972). Human behavior dynamics in a fire department. Fire Command, 39 (4), 36–39.

Caiden, G. E. (1977). Police revitalization. Lexington, MA: D. C. Heath and Co.

Caputo, P. (1977). Rumor of war. New York: Holt, Rinehart & Winston.

Cargill-Mazer, K. (1978). A rural Florida migrant health clinic: The research methodology. The Florida Journal of Anthropology, 3 (1), 34–45.

Chadorow, N. (1971). Being and doing: A cross-cultural examination of socialization of males and females. In V. Gornick and B. K. Moran (Eds.), Women in sexist society (pp. 259–291). New York: Basic Books.

Chapple, E. S. (1942). Rites of passage and rites of intensification. In E.S. Chapple & C. Coon (Eds.), Principles of anthropology. New York: Holt, Rinehart and Winston.

Chapple, E. S. & Coon, C. S. (1942). Principles of anthropology. New York: Holt, Rinehart and Winston.

Coles, R. (1976). Policemen complaints. In C. P. Potholm & R. E. Morgan (Eds.), Focus on police (pp. 213–224).

Conrad, J. (1960). The heart of darkness. Englewood Cliffs, NJ: Prentice Hall.

Corwin, R. (1969). Patterns of organization conflict. Administrative Science Quarterly 14, (4), 507–522.

Cottrell, W.F. (1940). The railroader. Stanford City, CA: Stanford University Press.

Cragen, J. F. (1975). Small group interaction and the fire service. Fire Command, 42 (7), 21–24.

Davis, K. & Papen, A. P. (1935). Youth in the depression. Chicago, IL: University Chicago Press.

Deakin, H. (1977). Firemen on the job. New Society, 42 (12), 465–466.

Dean, J. P. & Whyte, W. F. (1958). How do you know if the informant is telling the truth? Human Organization, 17 (1), 34–38.

Diesing, P. (1971). Patterns of discovery in the social services. Chicago, IL: Aldine Publishing.

Ditzell, P. (1976). Fire engines, firefighters: the men, equipment and machines from colonial days to the present. New York: Crown Publishers.

Dollard, J. (1949). Caste and class in a southern town. New York: Harper.

duToit, B. M. (1979). Stress crisis and behavior: A South African case. Journal of Modern African Studies, 17 (1), 117–140.

Eddy, E. M., & Partridge, W. L. (Eds.). (1978). Applied anthropology in America. New York: Columbia University Press.

Fasteau, M. F. (1974). The male machine. New York: McGraw-Hill

Fein, R. A. (1977). Examining the nature of masculinity. In A. G. Sargeant (Ed.), Beyond sex roles (pp.188–199). St. Paul, MN: West Publishing Co.

Finnerty, J. D. (1977). How often will firemen get their sleep? Management Science, 23 (11), 1169–1173.

Firth, R. (1964). Essays on social organization and values. London: The Athlore Press.

Fjelstad, M. A. (1978). Can a firefighter have a successful marriage? Fire Chief Magazine, 22 (8), 7677.

Florida State Abstract (1979)

Fried, E. (1971). Command at Fires: Part 1. Fire Chief Magazine, 2, 26–40.

Fried, E. (1971). Command at fires: Part II. Fire Chief Magazine, 3, 38–40.

Foster, G. M. and Anderson, B. G. Medical anthropology. New York: Wiley and Sons.

Gans, H. J. (1962). The urban villagers. New York: Free Press.

Gans, H. J. (1968). The participant observer as a human being: Observations on the personal aspects of fieldwork. In H. S. Becker et al. (Eds.), Institutions and the person, (pp. 300–317). Chicago, IL: Aldine Publishing Co.

Getz, M. (1978). Evaluating efficiency of fire departments. Atlanta Economic Review, 28 (4), 44–49

Goldberg, H. (1976). The hazards of being male. New York: Signet.

Golde, P. (1970). Women in the field. Chicago, IL: Aldine Publishing Co.

Goodchilds, J. A. (1972). On being witty: Causes, correlates and consequences. In J. H. Goodstein & P. E. McGhee (Eds.), The psychology of humor. New York: Academic Press.

Goodenough, W. H. (1978). Multi-culturalism as the normal human experience. In W. L. Partridge & E. Eddy (Eds.), Applied anthropology in America (pp. 79–86). New York: Columbia University Press.

Goodstein, L. D. & Sargeant, A. G. (1977). Psychological theories of sex differences. In A. G. Sargeant (Ed.), Beyond sex roles (pp. 201–218). St. Paul, MN: West Publishing Company.

Greenwood, J. G., Hill, R. F., & Stein, H. F. (1978). Role negotiation between PAs and MDs in rural primary care. Annual AAA meeting, Los Angeles, CA.

Grinker, R. R. & Spiegel, J. P. (1945). Men under stress. Philadelphia: Blakiston Press.

Gusfield, J. R. (1960) Fieldwork reciprocities in studying a social movement. In R. N. Adams & J. J. Preiss (Eds.), Human organization research: Field relations and techniques pp. (99–108). Homewoood, IL: Dorsey Press.

Gussow, Z. (1964) The observer-observed relationship as information about structure in small group research. Psychiatry, 27, 230–247.

Hall, E. T. (1966). The hidden dimension. New York: Doubleday.

Harper, W. R. (1974). Human factors in command and control for Los Angeles fire department. Applied Ergonomics, 5 (1), 26–35.

Harris, J. S. (1978). Organizational and psychological considerations of EMS in the fire department. International Association Fire Chiefs, 44 (12), 18–19.

Harrison, A. (1979) The rural fire chief: Who is he? The International Fire Chief, 45 (3), 14–18.

Hegge, F., Marlowe, D., Redmond, D. P., & Sing, H. C. (1979). Psychological and physiological factors in exposure to life threat: A pilot study. Unpublished research protocol, Walter Reed Army Institute, Bethesda, MD.

Henerson, M. E., Morris, L. L., & Fitz-Gibbon, C. T. (1978). How to measure attitudes. Beverly Hills, CA: Sage Publications.

Henley, N. & Thorne, B. (1977) Womanspeak and manspeak: Sex differences and sexism in communication, verbal and non-verbal. In A. G. Sargeant (Ed), Beyond sex roles (pp. 201–218). St. Paul, MN: West Publishing Co.

Hill, C. E. (1977). Anthropological studies in the American South: Review and direction. Current Anthropology, 18 (2), 309–326.

Honigman, J. J. (1976). Sampling in ethnographic fieldwork. In R. Naroll & R. Cohen (Eds.), A handbook of method in cultural anthropology (pp. 266–281). New York: Columbia University Press.

Honigman, J. J. (1976). The personal approach in cultural anthropology research. Current Anthropology, 17 (2), 243–261.

Hostetler, J. A. & Huntington, G. E. (1968) Communal socialization patterns in Hutterite society. Ethnology, 7 (10), 331–355

Hunt, E. E. (1978). Ecological frameworks and hypothesis testing in medical anthropology. In M. H. Logan and E. E. Hunt (Eds.), Health and the human condition (pp. 84–100). North Scituate, MA: Duxbury Press.

International Association of Firefighters. (1977). 1976 annual death and injury survey. Internal report,. Washington, D.C.

Jacobs, A. H. (1976). Volunteer firemen: Altruism in action. In W. Arens & S. Montague (Eds.), The American dimension: Cultural myths and social reality (pp. 194–205). New York: Alfred Publishing.

Janis, I. L., Jr. (1963). Group identification under conditions of external danger. Journal of Medical Psychology, 36, 227.

Kahn, R. L. (1969). Stress: From 9-5. Psychology Today, 3 (2), 34.

Karter, M. J., Jr. (1979). Firefighters injuries in the U.S. during 1978. Fire Command, 46 (12), 74–18.

Kennedy, J., & Stephan, W. G. (1977). The effects of cooperation and competition on ingroup-outgroup bias. Journal of Applied Social Psychology, 7 (2), 115–130.

Killian, L. (1970). White southerners. New York: Random House.

Kimball, W. Y. (1970). Fire department terminology. Boston, MA: National Fire Protection Association.

Kluckhohn, C. (1956). The influence of psychiatry on anthropology in America during the past 100 years. In D. G. Harding (Ed.), Personal character and cultural milieu (pp. 485–506) New York: Syracuse University Press.

La Barre, W. (1958). The influence of Freud on anthropology. American Image, 15, 275–328.

La Fontaine, J. S. (Ed.), (1972). The interpretation of ritual. London: Tavistock Publications.

Langness, L. L. (1965). The life history in anthropological science. New York: Holt, Rinehart & Winston.

Lawless, R. (1979). The concept of culture. Minneapolis, MN: Burgess Publications.

Leaf, M. J. (1974) Ritual and social organization: Sikh marriage rituals. In M. J. Leaf (Ed), Frontiers of anthropology (pp. 123–162). New York: Van Nostrand and Co.

LeFave, L. (1972). Humor judgements as a function of reference groups and identification classes. In J. H. Goodstein and P. E. McGhee (Eds.), The psychology of humor (pp. 195–210). New York: Academic Press.

LeMasters, E. E. (1975). Blue collar aristocrats: Life styles at a working class tavern. Madison, WI: University of Wisconsin Press.

Levinson, D. J., Darrow, C. M., Klein, E. B., Levinson, M. H., & McKee, B. (1977). Periods in the adult development of men: Ages 18–45. In A. G. Sargeant (Ed.), Beyond sex roles (pp.279–291). St. Paul, MN: West Publishing Co.

Lewin, M. A. (1976). Psychological aspects of minority group membership: The concepts of Kurt Lewin. In T. Blass (Ed.), Contemporary social psychology (pp. 128–137). Itasca, IL: Peacock Publishers.

Logan, M. H. & Hunt, E. E. (1978). Health and the human condition: Perspectives on medical anthropology. North Scituate, MA: Duxbury Press.

Lozier, J. (1976). Volunteer fire departments and community mobilization. Human Organization, 35 (4), 345–354.

Lundberg, C. C. (1968). A transactional conception of fieldwork. Human Organization, 27 (1), 45 49.

Makielski, S. J., Jr. (1975). The politics of change: Southern pluralism and ethnic identification. In J. W. Bennet (Ed.), The new ethnicity: Perspectives from ethnology (pp. 197–214). St. Paul, MN: West Publishing Co.

Martineau, W. H. (1972). A model of the social functions of humor. In J. H. Goodstein & P. E. McGhee (Eds.), The psychology of humor (pp. 101–125). New York: Academic Press.

Matarazzo, J., Allen, B., Saslo, G., & Wiens, A. (1964) Characteristics of successful policemen and firemen applicants. Journal of Applied Psychology, 48 (2), 123–133.

McCarty, D. (1975). Stress and the firefighter. Fire Command, 42, (1) 38–39.

Mead, M. (1970). Fieldwork in the Pacific Islands, 1925–1967. In P. Golde (Ed.), Women in the field (pp. 293–331). Chicago, IL: Aldine Publishing Co.

Miller, G. W., Presley, R. W., & Sniderman, M. S. (1973). Multi job holding by firemen and policemen compared. Public Personnel Management, 2 (4), 283–289.

Miller, J. M. (1976). Validation of a test for selecting firefighters. Doctoral dissertation, Marquette University, Marquette, WI.

Mills, T. M. (1970). Group structure and the newcomer. In T. M. Mills & M. J. Rosenburg (Eds.), Readings on the sociology of small groups (pp.149–164). Englewood Cliffs, NJ: Prentice Hall Publishers.

Mochon, M. J. (1974). Working class constraints and choices: An urban case study. Urban Anthropology, 3 (1), 47–63.

Molohan, K. T., Paton, R., & Lambert, M. (1979). An extension of Barth's concept of ethnic boundaries to include both other groups and developmental stage of ethnic groups, Human Relations, 32 (1), 1–17.

Murphree, A. (1976). The anatomy and physiology of a rural county. In R. C. Reynolds (Ed.), The health of a rural county: Perspective and problems (pp. 12–32). Gainesville, FL: University of Florida Press.

Nader, L. (1970). From anguish to exaltation. In P. Golde (Ed.), Women in the field. (pp. 97–116) Chicago, IL: Aldine Publishing Co.

Naroll, R. (1964). On ethnic unit classification. Current Anthropology, 5 (4), 283–312.

Neville, G. K. (1975). Kinfolks and the covenant: Ethnic community among southern Presbyterians. In J. W. Bennet (Ed.), The new ethnicity: Perspectives from ethnology (pp. 258–274). St. Paul, MN: West Publishing Co.

Niederhoffer, A. & Niederhoffer, E. (1978). The police family: From station house to ranch house. Lexington, MA: D. C. Heath and Co.

Novak, M. (1971). The rise of the unmeltable ethnics: Politics and culture in the seventies. New York: Macmillan Co.

Noyes, R. and R. Kletti. (1976). Depersonalization in the face of life-threatening danger: A description. Psychiatry, 39, 19–27.

Oliver-Smith, A. (1979). The crisis dyad: Meaning and culture in anthropology and medicine. In W. R. Rogers & D. Barnard (Eds.), Nourishing the humanistic in medicine: Interactions with the social sciences. Pittsburgh: University of Pittsburgh Press.

Olmsted, M. S. & Hare, A. P. (1978). The small group. New York: Random house.

O'Reilly, C. A. & Roberts, K. H. (1977). Task group structure, communication, and effectiveness in three organizations. Journal of Applied Psychology, 62 (6), 674–681.

Partridge, W. L. & Eddy, E. M. (Eds.), (1978). Applied anthropology in America. New York: Columbia University Press.

Pelto, P. J. & Pelto, G. H. (1978). Medicine, anthropology, community: An overview. In M. H. Logan and E. E. Hunt (Eds.), Health and the human condition (pp. 401–406). North Scituate, MA: Duxbury Press.

Pelto, P. J. (1974). Anthropological research: The structure of inquiry. New York: Harper and Row.

Pfifferling, J. H. (1978). Powerless power control by the anthropologist. Annual AAA Meeting, Los Angeles, CA.

Pierce, C. & Sanfacon, J. (1977). Man/woman dynamics: Some typical communication patterns. In A. G. Sargeant (Ed.), Beyond sex roles (pp.97–105). St. Paul, MN: West Publishing Co.

Polker, J. H. (1970). The image of the firefighter—is it changing? Fire Command, 37 (10), 16–18.

Pothaolm, C.P. and Morgan, R.E. (Eds). Focus on police. Cambridge, MA: Schenkman Publishing Co.

Powdermaker, H. (1966). Stranger and friend: The way of an anthropologist. New York: Norton Press.

Radcliffe-Brown, A. R. (1952). Structure and function in primitive society. London: Cohen & West Publishers.

Reed, J. S. (1972). The enduring south: Subcultural persistence in mass society. Chapel Hill, NC: University of North Carolina Press.

Richardson, F. L. W. (1978). The elusive nature of cooperation and leadership: Discovering a primitive process that regulates human behavior. In W. L. Partridge and E. M. Eddy (Eds.), Applied anthropology in America (pp. 87–111). New York: Columbia University Press.

Richardson, S. A. (1960). A framework for reporting field relations experiences. In R. M. Adams, & J. J. Preiss (Eds.), Human organization research (pp. 124–139). Homewood, IL: Dorsey Press.

Robbins, E. (1975). Ethnicity or class? Social relations in a small Canadian industrial community. In J. W. Bennet (Ed.), The new ethnicity: Perspectives from ethnology (pp. 285–304). St. Paul, MN: West Publishing Co.

Roebuck, J. & Quan, R. (1976). Health care practices in the American deep south. In R. Wallis & P. Morley (Eds.), Marginal medicine (pp. 141–161). New York: The Free Press.

Rosaldo, M. S. & Lamphere, L., (Eds). (1974). Women, culture and society. Stanford, CA: Stanford University Press.

Ross, J. K. (1975). Social borders: Definitions of diversity. Current Anthropology, 16, 53–72.

Rush, A. J., Hill, R. F., Stanhope, W. D., & Costiloe, P. (1977). A pilot study of injuries in firefighters: An assessment of psychological and social influences, Unpublished manuscript. Oklahoma City, OK: Oklahoma City Fire Department.

Sanders, I. T. & Lewis, G. F. (1976). Rural community studies in the United States: A decade in review. Annual Reviews, Inc., 35–53.

Schau, E. J. (1974). The development of forced-choice instruments to evaluate work performance of firefighters and paramedics and an examination of correlates of those instruments. Doctoral dissertation, University of Washington, Seattle.

Scott, W. R. (1963). Fieldwork in a formal organization: Some dilemmas in the role of observer. Human Organization, 22, (1) 162–168.

Selye, H. (1978). The stress of life. New York: McGraw-Hill Book Co.

Seybolt, J. W. (1976). Work satisfaction as a function of the person-environment interaction. Organizational Behavior and Human Performance, 17, 66–75.

Shaver, P., Schurtman R., & Blank, T.O., (1975). Conflict between fireman and ghetto dwellers: Environmental and attitudinal factors. Journal of Applied Social Psychology, 5 (3), 240–261.

Sheehy, G. (1977). Passages. New York: Bantam Books.

Shepard, H. A. Men in organizations: Some reflections. In A. G. Sargeant (Ed.), Beyond sex roles (pp. 387–394). St. Paul, MN: West Publishing Co.

Sherif, M. (1954). Integrating fieldwork and the laboratory in small group research. American Sociological Review, 19, 759–771.

Shields, D. (1974). Firefighters' self-image, projected image and public image. Fire Command, 41, (1) 26–27.

Smith, D. (1972). Report from Engine Co. 82. New York: Saturday Review Press.

Smith, D. (1976). The final fire. New York: Saturday Review Press.

Smith, D. & Freedman, J. (1978). Firehouse. Garden City, NJ: Doubleday.

Smith, E. E. & Goodchilds, J. D. (1963). The wit in large and small established groups. Psychology Reports, 13, 273–274.

Spradley, J. P & Phillips, M. (1972). Culture and stress: A quantitative analysis. American Anthropology, 74 (3), 518–529.

Stein, E. E. (1960). The eclipse of communities: An interpretation of American studies. Princeton, NJ: Princeton University Press.

Stephenson, J. B. & Greer, L. S. (1981). Ethnographers in their own cultures: Two Appalachian cases . Human Organization, 40 (2), 123–130.

Tanner, O. (1976). Stress. Alexandria, VA: Time-Life Publishers.

Tavris, C. & Offir, C. (1977). The longest war: Sex differences in perspective. New York: Harcourt, Brace.

Taylor, A. (1976). Women police officers and their husbands: Both wed to the force. In C. P. Potholm & R. E. Morgan (Eds.), Focus on police (pp. 207–212). Cambridge, MA: Schenkman Publishing Co.

Thibault, J. W. & Kelley, H. H. (1959). The social psychology of group. New York: Wiley and Sons.

Thomas, C. E. (1975). Fire service: Orientation and indoctrination. Washington, DC: IAFC/IAFF.

Tiger, L. (1969). Men in groups. New York: Random House.

Townsend, R. C. (1977). The competitive male as loser. In A. G. Sargeant (Ed.), Beyond sex roles (pp. 228–242). St. Paul, MN: West Publishing Co.

Tremitiedi, R. (1974). Occupational emotional stress and the firefighter. Fire Command, 41, (1) 27–28.

Turner, R. (1967). Types of solidarity in the reconstituting of group. Pacific Sociological Review, 10 (2), 60–68.

Turner, V. (1968) The drums of affliction. Oxford: Claredon Press.

Turner, V. (1969). The ritual process. Chicago, IL: Aldine Publishing Co.

Ulrich, R. L. (1970). The human factor in fire department management. Fire Command, 37, (11) 12–15.

van Gennep, A. (1960). The rites of passage. Chicago, IL: University of Chicago Press.

Vidich, A. J. & Bensman, J. (1960). Small town in mass society: Class, power and religion in a rural community. New Jersey: Princeton University Press.

Warheit, G. J. & Waxman, J. (1973). Operational and organizational adaptations of fire departments to civil disturbances. American Behavioral Scientist, 16 (3), 343–355.

Warner, W. L. (1959). The living and the dead. New Haven, CT: Yale University Press .

Warner, W. L. (1962). American life: Dream and reality. Chicago: University of Chicago Press.

Warren, R. I. (1972). The community in America. Chicago, IL: Rand McNally.

Wasylenko, M. J. (1977). Some evidence of elasticity of supply of policemen and firefighters. Urban Affairs Quarterly, 12 (3), 365–382.

Wax, M. L. (1977). On fieldworkers and those exposed to fieldwork: Federal regulations and moral issues. Human Organization, 36 (3), 321–328.

Wax, R. H. (1960). Reciprocities in researcher—informant relations: Reciprocity in fieldwork. In R. N. Adams & J. J. Preiss (Eds.), Human organization research: field relations and techniques (pp. 90–98). Homewood, IL: Dorsey Press.

Weller, J. M. (1973). Involuntary partisans—fire departments and threat of conflict. American Behavioral Scientist, 16 (3), 368–377.

Wheeler, H. N. (1977). Officers in municipal fire departments. Labor Law Journal, 28 (11), 721–733.

Whyte, W. F. (1955). Street corner society. Chicago, IL: University Chicago Press.

Whyte, W. F. (1957). On asking indirect questions. Human organization, 15 (1), 21–23.

Whyte, W. F. (1960). Interviewing in field research. In R. N. Adams & J. J. Preiss (Eds.), Human organization research: Field relations and techniques (pp. 352–374). Homewood, IL: Dorsey Press.

Whyte, W. F. (1970). Doc and his boys. In T. M. Mills & M. J. Rosenberg (Eds.), Readings on the sociology of small groups (pp. 128–137). Englewood Cliffs, NJ: Prentice Hall Publishers.

Whyte, W. F. (1978). Organizational behavior research-where do we go from here? In W. L. Partridge & E. M. Eddy (Eds.), Applied anthropology in America (pp. 129–146). New York: Columbia University Press.

Wolfe, L. (1964). Anthropology. Englewood Cliffs, NJ: Prentice-Hall.

Woods, J. (1975). Firecalls: Ethnography of firefighters. In J. P. Spradley & D.W. McCurdy (Eds.), The cultural experience: Ethnography in complex society (pp. 221–239). Chicago: Science Research Associates, Inc.

Woods, S. M. (1976). Some dynamics of male chauvinism. Archives of General Psychology, 33 (1), 63–65.

Yorburg, B. (1974). Sexual identity: Sex roles and social change. New York: Wiley and Sons.

Zaltman, R,. Duncan, R. & Holbek, J. (1973). Innovations and organizations. New York: Wiley and Sons.

APPENDICES

———

APPENDIX A
FIRE FIGHTERS' BASIC INFORMATION SHEET

General Instructions: Please do not put your name anywhere on this sheet. Please answer all the questions as fully as possible. If a question does not apply to you, please put N.A. (not applicable) in the blank. When finished, just put this sheet in the envelope, seal it and give it to me.

1. Are you a full-time paid fire fighter now or a volunteer?
   ____ paid   ____ volunteer

2. Age ____

3. Marital status: married ____   single ____
       4. How many times have you been married? ____
       5. Number of children? ____
       6. Ages of children? ____

7. Where were you born? _____

8. Where were you raised? _____

9. How long have you lived in north (state)? ____ years

Please <u>circle</u> the highest grade completed:
10. High school   1   2   3   4
11. Junior college   1   2
12. College   1   2   3   4
13. Technical school   1   2   3   4

14. Do you attend school or training classes now?
       yes ____   no ____

15. How many hours a week do you devote to school or to the training classes?   _____ hours per week

16. What special skills did you bring to your present job? (For example, are you a skilled mechanic, carpenter, etc). Please <u>check</u> the courses you have taken and <u>check</u> if you are certified.

	<u>YES</u>	<u>NO</u>	<small>CERTIFIED</small>
17. 30 Hour FF Course	____	____	____
18. Vehicle extraction	____	____	____
19. 200 Hour FF Course	____	____	____
20. First Aid	____	____	____
21. First Aid Instructor	____	____	____
22. ACLS	____	____	____
23. ACLS Instructor	____	____	____
24. CPR	____	____	____
25. CPR Instructor	____	____	____
26. EMT	____	____	____
27. EMT Instructor	____	____	____
28. Paramedic	____	____	____
29. Paramedic Instructor	____	____	____
30. Forest Fire Course	____	____	____
31. Hazardous Materials	____	____	____
32. Hazardous Materials Instructor	____	____	____
33. Forcible Entry	____	____	____
34. Breathing Apparatus	____	____	____
35. Fire Science Degree	____	____	____
36. School Bus Rescue	____	____	____
37. High Rise Rescue	____	____	____
38. Smokedivers	____	____	____

39. Other classes you have taken: _____

40. Classes you are taking now: _____

41. What is your present job title (for retired fire fighters, what was your highest rank?) _____

42. How long have you had this job?
    ____ years ____ months

43. How long have you (had you) worked at this station?
    ____ years ____ months

44. How many total years have you (had you) been a paid fire fighter? ____ years ____ months

45. If you left this department, would you like to work in: (check all answers that apply to you).
____ paid department   ____ rural (south)
____ a volunteer department   ____ urban (south)
____ a large dept. (60+ people)   ____ rural (north)
____ a small dept. (less than 60) ____ urban (north)

46. Referring to your answers to #45, please state why you chose the areas you did..

47. Were you ever a volunteer fire fighter? ____ yes ____ no

48. How long were you a volunteer? ____ years ____ months

49. What regular (paying) work besides fire fighting do you do?

50. About how many hours a week do you do these other jobs?
____ hours per week

51. Do you work for other people or are you self-employed?
____ work for others ____ self-employed

52. Do you now or have you ever had relatives who were fire fighters? ____ yes ____ no

53. Which of your relatives has been or is now a firefighter (either paid or volunteer)?
____ brother ____ sister   ____ father   ____ mother
____ nephew   ____ son   ____ uncle   ____ aunt
____ niece   ____ grandfather   ____ cousin
____ other (specify) _____

Thanks very much for helping me with my study. If you have any comments at all about this set of questions, please write them here.

APPENDIX B
WOMEN'S BASIC INFORMATION SHEET

General Instructions: Please do not put your name anywhere on this sheet. This basic information sheet is designed to help me get an idea of what it means to each of you to be married to or be going with a fire fighter. Will you answer each question as fully as possible. Please use the back of the paper if you want to. If a question does not apply to you, just put N.A. (not applicable) in the blank.

1. Age ____

2. Marital status: ____ married   ____ single
                   ____ divorced   ____ widow

3. How many times have you been married? ____ times

4. Number of children? ____ children
5. Ages of children? ____ ____ ____ ____ ____

Please <u>circle</u> the highest grade completed:
10. High school   1 2 3 4
11. Junior college   1 2
12. College   1 2 3 4
13. Technical school   1 2 3 4

10. Do you attend school or training classes now?
        yes ____   no ____

11. Have you ever taken any fire fighting classes?
        yes ____   no ____

12. If yes, which classes have you taken? _____

13. Would you like to take some fire fighting courses?
        ____ yes   ____ no

14. Have you ever taken any EMT/Paramedic courses?
        ____ EMT   ____ Paramedic   ____ neither one

15. Are you a certified EMT or Paramedic?
        ____ EMT   ____ Paramedic   ____ no, neither one

16. Would you like to take any EMT/Paramedic courses?
    ____ EMT ____ Paramedic ____ no, neither one

17. Please explain briefly why you would like to or why you
    you would not like to take fire fighting or EMT/Paramedic
    courses. _____

18. Do you have a job outside the home? ____ yes ____ no

19. If yes, what do you do? _____

20. If yes, how many hours do you work outside the home?
    ____ hours per week

21. If no, would you like to work outside the home?
    ____ yes ____ no

22. How do you schedule your work hours around those of
    your fire fighter?
    _____

23. Is the time you spend with your fire fighter sufficient?
    ____ yes ____ no

24. Would you like the fire department to provide more social
    activities for you to be part of? ____ yes ____ no

25. What activities would you like to see added at the station?
    _____

26. Would you participate in a women's auxiliary if one could
    be organized? ____ yes ____ no

27. What could a women's auxiliary do?
    _____

28. On a monthly average, do you and your fire fighter do
    more things with fire fighters or with non-fire fighters?
    ____ more with fire fighters ____ more with non-fire fighters

29. What do you like to do when you socialize with other fire fighters? (Please check all that apply to you).
____ church   ____ sports   ____ hunting ____ fishing
____ clubs   ____ school   ____ movies   ____ drinking
____ station events   ____ family events
____ other (please specify) _____

30. When your fire fighter is on duty, what do you personally like to do?
____ church   ____ sports   ____ hunting ____ fishing
____ clubs   ____ school   ____ movies   ____ drinking
____ station events   ____ family events
____ other (please specify) _____

31. What do you like to do when you both socialize with non-fire fighters?
____ church   ____ sports   ____ hunting ____ fishing
____ clubs   ____ school   ____ movies   ____ drinking
____ family events
____ other (please specify) _____

32. Who are the non-fire fighters you socialize with?
____ relatives   ____ friends   ____ both

33. What does your fire fighter like to do when you cannot join him?
____ church   ____ sports   ____ hunting ____ fishing
____ clubs   ____ school   ____ movies   ____ drinking
____ family events
____ other (please specify) _____

34. Do you now or have you ever had relatives who were fire fighters? ____ yes   ____ no

35. Which of your relatives has been or is now a fire fighter?
____ brother   ____ sister   ____ father   ____ mother
____ nephew   ____ son   ____ uncle   ____ aunt
____ niece   ____ grandfather   ____ cousin
____ other (specify) _____

36. Do you listen to the scanner when your fire fighter is on duty?
yes ____   no ____   don't own a scanner ____

37. If you own a scanner, why do you or why do you not listen?

38. Do you like to go to fire drills and watch?
yes _____   no _____

39. Why or why not?

40. What do you do when you go to the drills?

41. Do you like the fact that your man is a fire fighter?
yes _____   no _____

42. Do you like the work your fire fighter does?
yes _____   no _____

43. Why or why not?

44. Do you worry about your fire fighter when he is at a fire or on a rescue run?   yes _____   no _____

45. What worries you?

46. What do you do when you worry?

47. What does your fire fighter like best about what he does?

48. What does he like the least about what he does?

49. What do you discuss about his job with him?

50. What do you discuss about fire fighting with the other wives and girlfriends of fire fighters?

51. What did you think of these questions? If I have not asked about something you think is important, please add your comments below.

APPENDIX C
FIRE FIGHTERS' INTENSIVE INTERVIEW

General Instructions: (Read to each man before the interview begins). I want to ask you some questions about what it means to you to be a fire fighter. I would like to tape this interview, after which it will be typed up and the tape destroyed. The decision about whether or not the interview is taped is up to you. Again, please understand that your name and the name of the community will not be identified in the study. All of your answers are confidential. Is this alright with you?

1. How did you get interested in becoming a fire fighter?

2. What do you think makes a good fire fighter?

3. How do you know when you can trust a man in a fire situation?

4. Who would you want behind you on a charged line (name of a man or personal characteristics)?

5. If there were a rescue to be made, who would you follow into a fully involved structure fire to make that rescue (name a man or personal characteristics)?

6. Do you like your job?

7. What is the most hazardous part of your job?

8. Do you have the equipment necessary to meet those hazards?

9. What is the most enjoyable part of your work?

10. Why?

11. What is the most annoying part of your work?

12. What is the most physically stressful part of your job?

13. What is the most emotionally stressful part of your work?

14. How do you deal with the stress you feel?

15. What do you discuss with the other fire fighters about your work?

16. What do you think makes a good officer?

17. Of all the training you have had, what are you best at?

18. Can you train a man to be a good fire fighter or does it come naturally?

19. Can anyone learn to be a fire fighter?

20. What would you like more training in?

21. Do you ever worry about your safety on the job?

22. What specifically do you worry about?

23. What do you do when you worry?

24. Do you like running rescue?

25. Do you prefer running rescue to fighting fire?

26. Why or why not?

27. Are there problems at the station?

28. What are they?

29. How would you solve those problems?

30. What do you think of the seniority system?

31. What do you think about the system of reprimands?

32. What do you think about the Fire Fighters' Union?

33. Would a union work in this department?

34. What is an "attitude problem?"

35. How would you deal with an "attitude problem?"

36. Would you tell me about head flushing and the stretcher treatment?

37. What do you think about the help you get from the volunteers?

38. Is the time you spend with your wife sufficient?

39. Would you like the fire department to provide more social activities for both of you to participate in?

40. What activities would you like to see added?

41. Would you like for your wife (or girl friend) to participate in a women's auxiliary if one could be organized?

42. What could a women's auxiliary do?

43. On a monthly average, do you and your wife do more things with other fire fighters or with non-fire fighters?

44. What do you do when you socialize with other fire fighters?

45. When your wife is unable to join you, what do you like to do?

46. What do you do together when you socialize with non-fire fighters?

47. Are these non-fire fighters friends, relatives or both?

48. When you are on duty, what does your wife like to do?

49. Do you worry about your wife and family while you are at the station?

50. Can you tell me what you worry about?

51. How do you handle these worries?

52. What do you discuss with your wife about your work?

53. Do you like your wife (girlfriend) to come to the fire drills?

54. Why or why not?

55. Do you like your wife (girlfriend) to come to the fire and watch you work?

56. Why or why not?

57. Would you like your wife (girlfriend) to take a class in fire fighting?

58. Why or why not?

59. How about an EMT class or a paramedic class?

60. Why or why not?

61. What did you think about the questions I have just asked you?

62. Did I cover the topics you wanted to discuss?

Indexed Glossary

ACLS: Advanced Cardiac Life Support; the use of rescue procedures, involving the use of IVs, drugs and a defibrillator on heart attack victims. Page 91.

advance the lines: to move forward with hose lines filled with water at pressure. Page 99.

agitate: to provoke a reaction from another fire fighter. Page 83.

air packs: portable air supply strapped to the fire fighter's back; composed of an air tank, hose and face mask. Page 59.

attitude problem: a person variously described as a "know it all;" someone who does not fit into the group or who chooses not to follow the group norms. Page 65.

apparatus: fire equipment, namely the fire engines. Page 20.

bay (of the fire station): large room with garage doors both front and back, containing all fire apparatus and ambulances. Page 101.

BLS: Basic Life Support: page 93.

Big Bertha: the fire siren in Cows Crossing which is sounded at all major fires; means all fire fighters should respond to the fire as soon as possible; "we need all the help we can get." Page 27.

beeper: a pager, which is a compact, pocket carried radio receiver for providing one-way communication, used to direct fire fighters to emergencies within a limited area. Page 26.

bowed up: a postural threat or counterthreat taken by a man; chest is puffed out, shoulders back, arms straight and fists clenched. Page 83.

break bad (broke bad): to become verbally angry. Page 83.

buddy up: term used to describe two-man teams involved in fire suppression, search and rescue or other rescue procedures. Page 25.

bunker gear: an alternate term for the fire fighters' personal protective gear; term derived from habit of placing gear at the end of the bunk bed in the barracks. Page 24.

captain: ranking officer in a shift at the Cows Crossing Fire Department. Page 15.

catch the hydrant: phrase used to describe action of fire fighter who jumps off the tailboard of the engine with hose line and runs to hydrant for the hook up. Page 99.

charged line: a hose filled with water at pressure; lines were 1", 1.5", and 2.5" in diameter capable of up to 250 psi, 150 psi and 80 psi respectively. Page 65.

Committee: an *ad hoc* group of five or six senior fire fighters who initiate ritual processes at the fire station. Page 82.

CPR: Cardiopulmonary resuscitation; a system of controlled action which results in artificial breathing and circulation for victim. Page 84.

crispy critter: a burned person, usually dead. Page 102.

deluge gun: nozzle capable of spraying water at greater than 500 gpm mounted on portable platform and can be used from top of an engine as is done in Cows Crossing. Page 100.

EMT: Emergency Medical Technician; a person trained to save lives and to prevent or alleviate suffering. Page 12.

Engine 5: At Cows Crossing, it was a 1965 Ford chassis with a Ward LaFrance fire body on it; capable of carrying four to eight men. Page 99.

Engine 7: At Cows Crossing, it was a 1972 custom Ward LaFrance fire truck, capable of carrying six to eight men. Page 99.

engineer: person responsible for regulating the water flow from the hydrant through the engine to the fire fighters; second in command on a shift. Page 25.

fall out: term used to describe a fire fighter who is injured, overcome by smoke fatigue or who is sick. Page 95.

fireground: that area immediately surrounding the fire; area between the secured perimeter and the fire. Page 100.

fire rescue: rescue of a victim out of a structure fire. Page 64.

first in: the fire fighter who first enters a structure fire with a charged line; usually is one of two men on a hose team. Page 64.

fully involved: a structure fire in which a major portion of the building is in flames. Page 99.

get right (got right): to become provoked and to verbally defend oneself or to threaten another. Page 83.

hazardous materials incidents: chemical spills or fires resulting from chemical spills. Page 61.

head flushing: a ritual used by the fire fighters primarily as an initiation into the group. Page 138.

hose team: two men who operate a charged line. Page 86.

Hurst tool or the Jaws of Life: gasoline powered tool used to cut people out of vehicles; has crushing, tearing, ramming and cutting capabilities. Page 91.

instigate: to provoke a reaction from another person. Page 136.

Lizard Run: a non-emergency rescue call. Page 103.

mutual aid: help rendered by one fire department to another in a fire emergency or disaster; aid may be given across fire district lines. Page 72.

nozzleman: the forward man in a two man hose team; nozzlemen regulate the flow and spray pattern of water from the hose. Page 64.

paramedic: person with training in advanced life saving techniques; distinguished from an EMT by ability to administer drugs to victims; gives instructions to EMTs in the field. Page 62.

protective gear: the personal gear worn by the fire fighters; made up of helmet, coat, pants and boots. Page 24.

response time: the time it takes for the fire fighters to get to a fire or other emergency. Page 99.

riding partners: two men who team up for ambulance duty. Page 64.

rookie: the newest man at the fire station. Page 10.

running rescue: to be out on a rescue call in the ambulance. Page 88.

scanner: a device used to monitor fire, police, and rescue calls. Page 68

Signal 4: a dispatch code for a traffic accident. Page 103.

Signal 7: a dispatch code for a dead person. Page 103.

Signal 20: a dispatch code for a mentally ill or a combative person. Page 103.

Signal 25: a dispatch code for a fire. Page 25.

Signal 100: a dispatch code for a fire which can be handled with the equipment initially sent to the scene. Page 26.

Smokedivers: a class which teaches advanced fire fighters their physical and mental limits. Page 22.

standby system: a working system in which fire fighters are on duty for 24 hours, then are on standby for an additional 24 hours. Page 80.

stretcher treatment: a ritual used by the fire fighters to redress breaches in group norms. Page 138.

10-18: one of the ten signals used in radio dispatch meaning "respond to the emergency with all due speed." Page 112.

10-22: a radio dispatch which means "disregard this call." Page 103.

10-66: a radio dispatch which means "cancelled call." Page 103.

triage: the selection of patients for treatment and the order in which they should be treated. Page 103.

working fire: fire at which the fire fighters lay hose lines and use those lines to suppress the fire. Page 24.

Further Reading

Docherty, R.W. (1993) Stress in fire fighters: Situations, reactions and interactions. (Doctoral dissertation, Open University, England, 1993). Dissertation Abstracts International, 53, (9-B), 4989.

Fullerton, C.S., McCarroll, J. E., Ursano, R.J., & Wright, K. M. (1992). Psychological responses of rescue workers: Fire fighters and trauma. American Journal of Ortho-psychiatry, 62, (3), 371–378.

Goza-Macmullan, G. R. (1989). A path analysis of a job burnout model among fire fighters (Doctoral dissertation, University of North Texas, 1989). Dissertation Abstracts International, 49, (10-B), 4588.

Moran, C. (1990) Does the use of humor as a coping strategy affect stresses associated with emergency work? International Journal of Mass Emergencies and Disasters, 8 (3), 361–377.

Morgan, S.A. (1990). a path-analytic study of stress, job characteristics, commitment, and coping style in fire fighters (Doctoral dissertation, California School of Professional Psychology, Los Angeles, 1990). Dissertation Abstracts International, 50, (7-B), 3200.

Mullan, M. G. (1985). The relationship between objective and perceived work stressors: An exploratory study (Doctoral dissertation, Columbia University, New York, 1985). Dissertation Abstracts International, 46, (6-A), 1522.

Navarre, R. J. (1984). Stress and fire fighters (Doctoral dissertation, University of Toledo, Ohio 1984). Dissertation Abstracts International, 44 (12-B), 3969.

Simpson C. R. (1994). A Fraternity of danger: volunteer fire companies and the contradiction of modernization. American Sociological Association Conference paper.

Simpson, C. R. & Smith, D. M. (1987) The volunteer rural fire company: Community, male culture and modernization. Society for the Study of Social Problems Conference paper.